AN INTRODUCTION TO SUSTAINABLE DEVELOPMENT GOALS

PEP

Asia . Europe . Americas . Australia . Africa

AN INTRODUCTION TO SUSTAINABLE DEVELOPMENT GOALS

by

HIMANNSHU SHARMA & TINA SOBTI

Table of Contents

Introduction

The world is changing, the environment is changing and with this,
there's another imperative thing that's changing, us, the human
beings. Have you ever thought of the variations that are happening
around you? How many times you've ruminated about the actual
reasons behind the changes in the atmosphere, or in your society?
Let's be honest, we always crib about how frequently the weather is
changing or how bad it's getting, most of the people talk about the
injustice happening to many, we feel gloomy after looking at how badly
our planet or its people are being harmed with but what have we done
about it? Let us ask this, who's responsible for the harm being caused
to this planet and humanity? We need to be a little upfront here and
say that it's nobody else, but us who are the reason behind most of
the unfortunate and undesirable things happening to, and in this
beautiful home or planet 'Earth', which don't know since when is
bearing the pain, heat, and sadness and being destructed because of
us but still is continuing to provide shelter to end number of people
residing here who instead and unfortunately are damaging it
persistently.

It's time to wake up and take charge for the purpose of bringing a
much-needed transformation before it's too late, there's already
enough destruction caused to the environment, society and its people
but the good news is that there's still a scope of augmentation and
this is what this book has been created for, it has been written for the
purpose of bringing you closer to the most virtuous solutions that can
turn things around if worked upon in an unsurpassed manner.
'Sustainable Development' is a pathway that can lead us towards an
enormous future and bring in an amazing transformation in the society
as well as environment. Yes, it can bring an astonishing revolution in
the environment and society if we all will start working towards it,
however, understand that we'll not be able to do this without gaining

an appropriate and in-depth understanding about the same.

It's imperative for us to comprehend what Sustainable Development is, and how can it help us in bringing the desired change in this world, healing the harm and misery caused to humanity and environment, and above all enable you to make this planet a wonderful home for all.

Also, remember that its not a one-man show, and we'd need a team to do this, in fact, we all need to join hands and ensure that every possible thing is done so that it can help us save this beautiful planet and all its wonderful beings. There are many activities given in each chapter which needs to be conducted by the students for the purpose of promoting each goal, however, this doesn't mean that they need to restrict themselves to these activities only. Novices must involve themselves in other research-based activities and encourage their peers to be a part of the same, the more the merrier. The idea is to promote each goal as much as possible so that end number of people can be motivated to work towards the Global Goals and be a part of this fantastic movement of creating a sustainable present and future for all.

Chapter – One

The Evolution of Sustainable Development

The concept of Sustainable Development came into existence in the year 1992 during Earth Summit in Rio de Janeiro and laid a foundation of United Nations Conference on Environment and Development. This was the summit wherein various plans and strategies were created to work upon for creating a sustainable way of living for all. This conference was attended by more than 100 state heads and representatives from approximately 178 national governments. Not only this, many people who represented civil societies and were an imperative attribute of congruent organisations also attended this summit.

In this summit, an enormous discussion took place which was to ruminate on various factors that could justify the need for Sustainable Development. Butland Commission in the year 1987 prepared a report which proved that Sustainable Development was immensely required to overcome various problems of environmental degradation. This report was prepared after doing a lot of research work to investigate the problems or issues faced by people in past decades, it also inculcated various means by which people were leaving a severe and negative impact on the environment and this planet. An imperative realisation came through this research that the patterns of growth and development would not remain sustainable if they'll remain unseen or unchecked.

Sustainable Development gained its first international recognition in the year 1972 at the United Nations Conference which was based on Human Environment and was held in Stockholm. The international community was convinced with this notion that Sustainable Development will be beneficial for the development of humanity and environment.

This concept was popularised 15 years later, and a classic definition of Sustainable Development was created & included in the report of World Commission on Environment:
"Development which meets the needs of the present without compromising the ability of future generations to meet their own needs."

The most recent summit on Sustainable Development was held in Johannesburg in the year 2002 which was attended by 191 national governments, myriad UN agencies, and other multilateral financial institutions along with some renowned international groups who altogether came together to assess the progress of Sustainable Development since Rio. This summit finalised various outcomes or key pointers which were supposed to be worked upon in order to work on the sustainable demand and supply, energy and water and sanitation, the major key pointers were enormous collaborative initiatives, execution of the Johannesburg plan of implementation and political declaration.

The Sustainable Development is depended upon three major attributes and they are economic, social and environmental development and we need to work upon each of them to ensure that we're able to do justice to this concept. There were 17 goals created in order to ensure the progress of Sustainable Development, these are known as Sustainable Development Goals or SDG. Let's look at views of some of the famous personalities on few of the Global goals:

"We, the present generation, have the responsibility to act as a trustee of the rich natural wealth for the future generations. The issue is not merely about climate change; it is about climate justice." - Narendra Modi.

"What we are doing to the forests of the world is but a mirror reflection of what we are doing   to ourselves and to one another." - Mahatma Gandhi.

"India should walk on her shadow – we must have our own development model". - A.P.J Abdul Kalam.

"Freedom cannot be achieved unless women have been emancipated from all forms of oppression". - Nelson Mandela.

"Education is pre – eminently a matter of quality, not amount" - Henry Ford.

"We shall not defeat any of the infectious diseases that plague the developing world until we have also won the battle for safe drinking water, sanitation, and basic health care". - Kofi Annan

The drive of making this world a healthy and safe home for all was not initiated with Sustainable Development Goals, before them came the Millennium Development Goals which were created with a congruent intent of making our planet immensely sustainable and virtuous for present as well as upcoming generations. Let's understand about these goals in detail in the next chapter.

Chapter – Two

The Millennium Development Goals

About Millennium Development Goals:

On 8th September 2000, leaders of 189 countries gathered at the United Nations Headquarters and signed the historic Millennium declaration, this declaration had eight objectives which were adopted by these countries and their leaders during this summit which aimed at achieving the following goals.

1. Eradicating Extreme Poverty and Hunger (MDG 1)

2. Achieving Universal Primary Education (MDG 2)

3. Promoting Gender Equality and Empowering Women (MDG 3)

4. Reducing Child Mortality (MDG 4)

5. Improving Maternal Health (MDG 5)

6. Combatting HIV/AIDS, Malaria and other diseases. (MDG 6)

7. Ensuring Environmental Sustainability (MDG 7)

8. Developing a Global Partnership for Development (MDG 8)

These Millennium Development Goals helped approximately one million people to come out of poverty, hunger and enabled myriad girls in getting themselves educated by attending school.

The hits and misses of Millennium Development Goals:

According to the Millennium Development Goals Report 2015, following are the accomplishments and weaknesses of the Millennium Development Goals:

MDG 1: Eradicating Extreme Poverty and Hunger: The extreme poverty rate was reduced from 1.9 billion in the year 1990 to 836 million in 2015 on a global level. The target of providing food and nutrition to maximum number of people, unfortunately, could not be achieved. However, the percentage of unnourished people in most of the developing regions which was 23.3 percent in the year 1990 was reduced to 12.9 percent in 2014.

MDG 2: Achieving Universal Primary Education: The goal of achieving universal primary education was missed but on the positive side, the enrolments of Primary Schools showed a remarkable upsurge, in 2000 the figure was 83 per cent which has now been increased up to 91 per cent this year in most of the developing regions.

MDG 3: Promoting Gender Equality and Women Empowerment: Approximately two third of the developing countries were able to achieve the objectives of attaining gender equality and education for all. The progress was immensely impressive in Southern Asia wherein in 1990 only 70 girls for every 100 boys were enrolled in a school and recently the number has increased, today there are 103 girls enrolled for every 100 boys.

MDG 4: Reducing Child Mortality: On a global level the mortality rate has been reduced by more than half since 1990 which means that the number of deaths which were 90 per cent have reduced to 43 per cent per 1000 births. However, if we look at it practically, around 16000 children who are less than the age of 5 are still dying from the causes which are easily preventable.

MDG 5: Improving Maternal Health: The great news is that the maternity mortality ratio has been reduced up to half with the help of Millennium Development Goals, however, there were around 2,89,000 deaths in the year 2013 due to the non-accomplishment of MDG 4.

MDG 6: Combatting HIV/AIDS, Malaria and other Diseases: The results are mixed when it comes to this goal, the target of eliminating HIV/AIDS has not been attained although the percentage has decreased between 2000 – 2013, it has now been reduced by 40 per cent. According to the United Nations Report, the global malaria incident rate has been reduced by 37 per cent resulting in the lessening of the mortality rate by 50 per cent.

MDG 7: Ensuring Environmental Sustainability: The quality of drinking water has been augmented between the year 1990 and 2015. 2.6 billion people have been given access to a better quality of water which means if we look at the worldwide statistics, almost half of the population has been given an access to drink an improved water. Not only this, around 2.1 billion people have been given an access to enhanced sanitation.

MDG 8: Developing a Global Partnership for Development: The assistance on development provided from the wealthy countries to developing ones have been increased by 66 per cent between the year 2000 and 2014, the exact number is of $ 135.2 billion.

The Next Step:

The 17 Sustainable Goals are the successor of Millennium Development Goals, which aim to build a more healthy, prosperous, equal and secure world by the year 2030. 193 state members at the United General Assembly which were held in September 2015 agreed to work upon the 17 SDG's and 169 targets which are a part of the 2030 Agenda for sustainable development, these goals came into effect on 1st January 2016.

All the countries, businesses and people or organisations working in the collaborative partnership are expected to work on this agenda which has been created to transform the world.

The World Vision believes that sustainable development embarks upon when the nourishment, education, and security of children are taken care of, they must be kept away from violence. SDG's have the potential to make this possible and it's responsible for each individual to work towards these goals and transform myriad lives along with bringing a much-required change in the society and environment.

The Global Goals are actually a universal call for people to come forward and act in order to end poverty, not only this, they encourage individuals to take all the necessary steps which can help them enjoy peace and prosperity. These goals also aim towards the protection of planet and hold some of the common targets as Millennium Development Goals, however, there are myriad new aspects added in these goals such as climate change, innovation, sustainable consumption, peace and justice and many other which can make this world a better place to live in for the future generation.

SUSTAINABLE DEVELOPMENT **GOALS**

17 GOALS TO TRANSFORM OUR WORLD

#SDGSketch

is a project by @Club17Africa http://club17africa.org in collaboration with @xLentras and @DrMinaOgbanga

SDGs is a UN program.

https://sustainabledevelopment.un.org

From the website:

"On September 25th 2016, countries adopted a set of goals to END POVERTY, PROTECT THE PLANET and ENSURE PROSPERITY FOR ALL as part of a new Sustainable Development Agenda..."

"For the Goals to be reached, Everyone needs to DO THEIR PART."

Aim of #SDGSketch PrJ is to create AWARENESS!!

SDGs improve KNOWLEDGE on SDGs amongst YOUTHS

17 GOALS & 169 TARGETS

↳ 17 Sketchnotes

Chapter – Three
The Sustainable Development Goals

The Global Goals were created in the year 2015 and launched by the United Nations, these were some of the most imperative targets which aimed towards fighting inequality, enhancing the current climatic conditions, eliminating poverty and a lot more and all these targets were given a shape keeping in mind that they'll be achieved till 2030. They came into effect in Jan'16 and are expected to be continued to work upon by 2030.

These goals are essential for the sustainability of not only our society but even this planet and if these targets will be achieved as per the plan, then it will bring immense health and safety for it as well as the ones living here. However, the only thing that can help in the 100 percent achievement of these goals is awareness of each and every individual and their contribution towards accomplishing them. These goals are actually a universal call to every person who is a part of this world to come forward, take charge and make this planet a wonderful and safe home for all.

Global Goals are the successors of Millennium Development Goals with an addition of new areas which weren't really included in MDG's. All these goals are interconnected which means that the success of one depends on handling the issues of the other. Some of the major reasons for creating the Global Goals are:

1. Ensuring peace on the governmental and democratic level.

2. Working towards economic inequality and climate change.

3. Eliminating poverty.

Achievement of these goals requires the partnership of various governments, citizens, the private sector, civil societies who altogether can ensure that this world becomes a safe place and this planet becomes a safe home for the present and upcoming generations.

Role of UNDP:

UNDP (United Nations Development Program) agency work towards the implementation of Global Goals by working with 170 countries and territories to eliminate poverty, inequality and accelerating the progress attained with the help of Millennium Development Goals. At present the accomplishments attained with the help and contribution of UNDP showcases that there's a possibility of Global Goals to be attained by the year 2030 however, they can't do this alone and need the support of myriad governments, societies and citizens in order to accomplish their targets aptly.

You can refer to the link given below in order to know more about the achievements and contribution of UNDP:

http://www.undp.org/content/undp/en/home/sustainable-development-goals/resources/

The need for Global Goals (SDG's):

The Global Sustainable Development Goals are required and imperative to be worked upon because of reasons given below:

1. There are more than 1 billion people who don't have access to fresh water.

2. An interesting fact which may encourage people to work towards SDG's is that if people worldwide would switch to light bulbs that are energy efficient it would help the word to save approximately 120 US dollars annually.

3. The leading cause of death among adolescents in Africa is AIDS.

4.   On an average 1 out of 5 people in the world are not provided with an access to modern electricity.

5.   1 out of 3 people does not have access to basic sanitation services.

6.   Approximately 1.5 billion people across the globe do not have access to reliable telephone services.

7.   In the year 2011, the rate of children leaving primary school affected almost 50 percent countries.

8.   80 percent of people living in rural areas still depend on the medicines extracted from plants in order to attain a basic health care.

9.   A High rate of primary school children attend their classes without taking proper nutrition which leaves them with a hungry stomach.

10.   828 people live in the slums and the number is rising constantly.

11.   The rate of unemployment increased from 170 million in 2007 to nearly 202 million in 2012.

12.   40 percent of the world oceans are affected by human activities.

Why are SDG's considered to be better than MDG'S?

1.   The Millennium Development Goals were majorly determined by the international donor agencies whereas SDG's are more globally collaborative than them. These goals are universal and considered to be holistic.

2.   The private sector was not much engaged in Millennium Development Goals however it is more engaged in the Sustainable Development Goals because of the initiatives after UN Global Compact, and now this sector has an enormous role to play in the achievement of Global Goals.

3. The Sustainable Development Goals are successors of Millennium Development Goals and are created with a motive of leaving no one behind.

4. The Global Goals are more inclusive in comparison to the Millennium Development Goals.

Please refer to the resource given below for more information:

https://www.theguardian.com/global-development-professionals-network/2015/sep/26/7-reasons-sdgs-will-be-better-than-the-mdgs

The world leaders agreed to work upon 17 goals in 2015 to fight poverty and gender inequality, stop climate changes and many other issues which are reasons behind the destruction of our society and planet. Let's look at each one of them in detail:

SUSTAINABLE DEVELOPMENT **GOALS**   #SDGSketch

17 GOALS TO TRANSFORM OUR WORLD

is a project by @Club17Africa http://club17africa.org in collaboration with @xlontrex and @DrMinaOgbanga

GOAL 1: End poverty in all its forms everywhere

By 2030

No more EXTREME POVERTY

50% LESS People living in POVERTY

MOVE RESOURCES from various sources to make them AVAILABLE to END POVERTY

Run systems to FIND, MEASURE and TRACK POVERTY

All men and women, in particular the poor and the vulnerable, have EQUAL RIGHTS to ACCESS ECONOMIC RESOURCES and BASIC SERVICES

PROTECT the Poor to EXTREME CLIMATE and other Shocks and Disasters

Create a sound policy framework based on strategies that look after the POOR and GENDER-SENSITIVE to facilitate investments in Actions to End Poverty

info: https://sustainabledevelopment.un.org/sdg1

GOAL 1: NO POVERTY

Eliminating poverty is not something to be considered as charity as every individual has a right to live above the poverty line, so it's a matter of justice. It helps an individual to unlock the power of humanity and enable others to come out of their misery. The sad part is that although many people are working towards this goal and despite of the efforts made by them, half of the world's population is still living in poverty, there are enormous people across the globe who are deprived of eating healthy food and drinking clean water. Hence this goal aim towards creating measures which can help in the elimination of every thing that is causing poverty in any city or country and not letting its people live a life which they truly deserve.

1.1 Significance of the goal 'Eliminating Poverty':

Meeting   Global Goals will certainly help us in eliminating or ending poverty and here are few of the targets we all must work upon to put an end to it:

1. Make it a point to eliminate poverty by the year 2030.

2. Jobs must be created for helping people to get a source of income and once they'll get one, it will become easier for them to come out of poverty.

3. We must pay attention towards Women Education, girls should be encouraged to be educated instead of getting married at a very young age. They should be made aware of various economic opportunities and must be heartened to work towards them.

4. Clean water and sanitation must be provided to poor people as this will help them save the time of fetching water from

different places and utilise it in their jobs or education. This could also reduce the healthcare burden as well.

5. Proper Nutrition must be provided to infants so that they can refrain themselves from developing any physical or mental disorder which could become a reason behind their poverty.

6. Health Insurances must be provided to poor people so that they can save money on expensive treatments.

7. People living in poverty must be helped to understand that they can come out of their condition and must be shown appropriate ways which could enable them to overcome the scarcity.

8. Financial Services must be provided to the poor people which could help them to start a small business for   augmenting their family income.

9. We could also help people to get rid of poverty by teaching them various skills which can help them get a job in the future.

10. Helping children from a low-income background to get admissions in schools so that they can get an appropriate education.

1.2. Reasons behind eliminating poverty:

1. **Good Education and Healthy Diet:** Children who grow up in poverty do not get an opportunity to get proper education and hence their chances of earning a good income reduces up to a great extent. Also, they don't get a proper diet which affects their health in an adverse manner. Once poverty will be eliminated from our society, these children will get an opportunity to acquire a virtuous education and a healthy diet.

2. **Reduction of Health Risks:** Once people will be provided with a healthy diet, the chances of them suffering from disorders and diseased will be reduced. Which will enable them to work efficiently and e

3. **Enhance the bond between family members**: Lack of money and resources can lead to various psychological issues which may affect the lives of family members who are living in poverty. So, the elimination of it would give them peace of mind and would enhance their relationship with each other.

Apart from these, there are many other reasons which encourage people to work towards the elimination of poverty. You can read about them on various social media platforms, or search about them on internet in order to acquire more knowledge about the same.

1.3 Student Involvement in promoting the goal No Poverty:

1. Students must help their peers (the ones from low income background) to be a part of all the extracurricular activities and ensure that they are treated equally as the ones from wealthy background.

2. 'Sharing and Caring' is one of the best things which can help novices to work towards eliminating poverty, you must keep a stock of eatables, snacks, clothes, medicines and other necessities and donate them to the ones who need these things more than you.

3. Run a campaign on 'Education for all' and make everyone aware about the significance of education for everyone. Performing Street Shows is one of the most interesting things you could do to draw attention of myriad people towards this goal.

4. Create awareness about this issue with the help of social media and motivate people to work towards it.

5. Students can perform an activity called 'Hunger Awareness Campaign' wherein they can pay a visit to places where people are living in extreme poverty. They can then prepare a project report and write solutions which can help them eliminate it from the society. These solutions can be

implemented with the help of teachers so that the best results can be attained.

6.   Another activity which can help students as well as teachers to work towards the elimination of poverty is 'Sole Challenge'. In this activity, each one will give up on one thing which they may not have if they would have been living in poverty.

7.   Welfare Food Challenge is also a wonderful activity wherein the students and teachers will take up a challenge for a week to eat food as per the income of people who are living in poverty. And the money saved in this week can be utilised for charity, sharing snacks or food items with poor people, or anything else which could help them in eliminating poverty from their area.

8.   Various documentaries or short movies can be played in the class rooms which can enhance the knowledge of students on this issue.

9.   Set up displays related to this goal and create awareness in your school about the same. You can paint T shirts, create posters, put up banners and a do a lot of creative things to create awareness pertaining to the goal 'No Poverty'. Conducting a class assembly on this is also a virtuous idea to spread awareness about this in your school.

SUSTAINABLE DEVELOPMENT GOALS

#SDGSketch

17 GOALS TO TRANSFORM OUR WORLD

is a project by @Club17Africa http://club17africa.org in collaboration with @Lontrax and @DrMinaOgbange

GOAL 2: End hunger, achieve food security and improved nutrition and promote sustainable agriculture

Food for EVERYONE all year long

STOP MALNUTRITION

More INVESTMENTS & INTERNATIONAL COOPERATION

Rural Infrastructures

Agricultural Research

BY 2030

DOUBLE agriculture productivity & INCOME of small-scale FOOD PRODUCER

FAIR WORLD AGRICULTURAL MARKET

Correct and Prevent trade restriction and distortion

Proper functioning of food commodity markets

By 2020 MAINTAIN GENETIC DIVERSITY of SEEDS

×2 ×2

SUSTAINABLE PRODUCTION SYSTEM

Access to food markets INFORMATION

LIMIT EXTREME FOOD PRICE VOLATILITY

GOAL NO. 2: ZERO HUNGER

Hunger, these days is one of the leading causes of death in the world. There are enormous resources available for everyone in the world, however the lack of their access and proper distribution leads to individuals survive without the consumption of proper nutrition which in turn has become a reason behind malnutrition. If we'll work towards global goals and promote sustainable agriculture with the help of advanced techniques and ensure proper and equal distribution of resources, then there's a high possibility of people not dying because of hunger.

2.1 Eliminating the problem of 'Hunger':

Following are the targets which we all need to work upon in order to make sure that proper food and nutrition is provided to maximum number of people across the globe:

1. We need to make sure that people have access to safe and healthy nutrition across the globe.

2. We must join hands and work towards eliminating malnutrition from the world.

3. Credit must be provided to poor countries so that people living their can start something of their own which can enable them to get proper food and nutrition.

4. Decent amount of donations must be made to various organisations which support and work towards this cause.

5. Farmers must be pushed towards Urban Farming.

6. An access to education must be given to myriad pupils, as it will enable them to be competent enough in the future and

earn a decent income required for living a healthy lifestyle and consuming a healthy diet.

7. Awareness must be created about birth – control as many people across the globe are not acquainted with contraceptives which can help them to plan their family aptly.

8. Empowering women to be educated is important so that they can be a helping hand and get good jobs in order to augment the condition of their family.

2.2 Reasons behind eliminating World Hunger:

Following are some of the reasons due to which World Hunger must be eliminated:

1. There are around 795 million people in the world who are unable to get proper food and a nutritious diet.

2. The death rates are high in children and the reason behind this is, lack of healthy diet and nutrition.

3. There are 66 million children in the world who go to school with a hungry stomach which cause lack of concentration and lower immunity in them and in turn affect their academics adversely.

4. Poor nutrition affects the physical and mental development of an individual hence we must help a maximum number of people in getting a healthy diet.

5. One - third of the food which is produced worldwide is wasted and hence doesn't reach people who need it the most.

2.3. Student's Involvement in Eliminating World Hunger:

If schools and students will promote the importance of healthy nutrition and work towards it then it can certainly create wonders beyond the classroom and bring an astounding change in the society, or perhaps in the world. Most of the novices must learn the significance of healthy eating in their school and through their teachers, these children must also be encouraged to spread this awareness as much as possible in order to ensure that end number of people can get access to a healthy diet. Here are some of the ways by which schools and students can eliminate World Hunger and help people improve their health by providing them with healthy nutrition:

1. **Fund Raising Campaigns**: Students with the help of teachers can organise various fund-raising campaigns inside and outside the campus and use the money generated in providing food to numerous children and adults who don't have access to healthy diet and nutrition.

2. **Raise your Voice:** Children must try and create awareness about consuming a healthy diet and fighting malnutrition in the nearby villages or areas wherein people are striving hard to get proper food, people there must be made aware about the importance of education and explained that how it can help them in improving the condition of their family.

3. **'Fight Against World Hunger' Movement:** This particular movement can be started on the social media and a good number of people must be encouraged to join hands with the school and its students and work towards eliminating World Hunger.

4. **Food Bank:** Schools with the help of students and teachers can create a Food Bank wherein they can spread awareness about reducing the wastage of food and can share their details with people to encourage them in contacting the school and its students to make food donations which can be distributed by children and teachers among those who need it the most. Novices and teachers

can also create food banks near their residences and carry on this activity there on a regular basis.

SUSTAINABLE DEVELOPMENT **GOALS** #SDGSketch

is a project by @Club17Africa http://club17africa.org in collaboration with @xLontrex and @Dr.MinaOgbanga

17 GOALS TO TRANSFORM OUR WORLD

GOAL 3: Ensure healthy lives and promote well being for all at all ages

*By 2030

100.000 LIVE BIRTHS

*Global Maternity Mortality Ratio down to less than 70 per 100.000

70

*Neonatal Mortality at least as low as 12 per 1000

1.000 LIVE BIRTHS

Under-5 Mortality at least as low as 25 per 1000

42 — 25

Universal Health-Care COVERAGE

IMPLEMENT **FCTC** WHO Framework Convention for Tobacco Control

Reduce deaths from hazardous pollution and contamination

By 2020, 50% less Global deaths and injuries by car accidents

End Epidemics

Universal access to sexual and reproductive health-care services

Premature mortality from non-communicable diseases

*Reduced by 1/3

Strengthen prevention and treatment of SUBSTANCES ABUSE

Support R&D of Vaccines and Medicines

Finance Health workforce growth in developing countries

Improve • early warning • risk reduction • management of Health Risks

GOAL 3: GOOD HEALTH AND WELL BEING

The aim of this particular goal is to ensure a healthy living and encouraging people to attain virtuous   well being. If we look at the data of last 15 years, it is found that the death rates among children have been reduced to almost half which in turn brings an awareness that attaining good health and well being is not difficult. However, the sad part is that despite of the availability of myriad measures, we are spending a huge amount of money as well as resources on treating those illnesses which are easily preventable. The purpose of this goal is to promote the significance of healthy living and promoting various measures which can help individuals to stay healthy and enjoy an appropriate state of well being.

3.1 The Significance of this goal:

Following are the reasons which can help you understand the significance of good health and well being, it is important for you to understand them because you can promote and encourage other's to be healthy only when you have appropriate knowledge about the same:

1.   This goal encourages people to take care of their health will help them to sustain and develop their physical, mental and emotional health and it will also improve their overall well being which in turn will make them feel good and healthy.

2. Good Health and Well Being promotes the cause of healthy eating and exercising on a regular basis. Eating appropriate diet along with regular workouts or physical exercises will enable individuals to remain fit as it will lower down the chances of them becoming

overweight. Not only this, it will boost their immune system and ensure that they do not develop any chronicle disease or disorder.

This goal promotes the importance of   overall well being of an individual, and when people will start working towards it they will notice an amazing change in their personality. Also, it encourages people to refrain themselves from getting involved in undesirable activities that can harm their health.

3.2 The targets to be achieved:

Following are the targets of goal 'Good Health and Well Being', the students along with their mentors must work together for their accomplishment:

1.   Creating awareness in people about ways to fight communicable diseases.

2.   Reducing mortality from non - communicable diseases.

3.   Preventing and treating substance abuse.

4.   Striving hard and working towards reducing road injuries and death.

5.   Reducing illness caused by harmful chemicals and pollution.

6.   Try and convince people to say 'No' to tobacco.

7.   Making people aware of global health risks.

3.3. Start with yourself before spreading the word:

Consuming a healthy diet or nutrition, exercising daily and performing congruent activities can keep us not only healthy but even help us live a stress - free and relaxed life as they reduce the risk of us being affected by any chronicle disease. It is important for most of the teenagers to eat a healthy diet so that their mind and body can develop appropriately. However, the situation is vice versa these days, many children are dwelling upon unhealthy eating habits and routine which is affecting their health adversely. It is important that not only children but even adults understand the need of living a healthy lifestyle, and must follow the below given steps in order to eliminate an unhealthy style of living and you must remember that every change begins from the self, so before you go ahead and ask your peers and other people to work towards this goal, you need to first start with yourself and here's how you can do this:

1. **Change your habits:** The first step of attaining good health is to introspect and find out what bad habits you have that are keeping you away from attaining a good health and well being and once you're done with this then take necessary steps to overcome the challenges that are keeping you away from being healthy. You can take help of your friends, teachers, parents or anybody whom you can trust and who can help you overcome your bad habits. The point is to stop doing anything which is causing harm to your health.

2. **Replace your unhealthy habits with healthy ones:** This is related to the first point, you must replace your unhealthy habits with healthy ones because till the time you do that you won't be able to experience good health and well being.

3. **Visualise a change in yourself:** Every change starts with a thought so once you feel determined about attaining good health start visualising yourself in your mind doing all the activities which can bring you closer to a healthy living. The more you'll visualise and train your mind to focus on these activities the faster you'll experience a change in your health and personality.

4. **Put a stop to negative conversations:** You need to stop thinking negative and understand the significance of good health and well being while bringing a change in yourself. There will be times when negative thoughts may strike your mind and try to

stop you from achieving your goals, that's the point where you have to act smart and take charge. Do everything possible to stay steady on the path of healthy living and create a wonderful life.

5. **Know that it is going to take time:** No habit can be changed with a snap of fingers and takes time and continuous efforts. It is important to be patient and persistent while changing your habits, give yourself time to change and once you'll do this, things will change automatically.

6. **General tips to keep yourself healthy:** Here are few of the tips you must remember if you wish to experience a good health and well being:

   A. Think positive and be thankful for all that you have.

   B. Eat green vegetables.

   C. Take 5 small meals instead of doing overeating.

   D. Get into a habit of exercising regularly.

   E. Take a proper 8 hours of sleep.

   F. Avoid consuming supplements and eat natural fruits and vegetables.

   G. Be around good friends, especially the ones who can help you become a good and healthy person.

   H. Try and meditate in order to relax your mind and body.

   I. Do not involve yourself in activities that create pollution.

   J. Refrain yourself from getting into a habit of smoking, eating tobacco etc.

3.4 Student's involvement in promoting the goal 'Good Health and Well Being':

Students can conduct the following activities with the help of their mentors in order to encourage their peers and other people to work towards the goal Good Health and Well Being:

1. **Creating Comic Strips:** You can create interesting comic strips based on this particular goal and convey your message through it, once it is designed circulated it in your school as well as people residing in the nearby areas.

2. **Plate and Planet:** This is an activity wherein you will be required to encourage people to acquire a habit of healthy eating, be as creative as possible and enjoy it with your peers. You can also visit the areas nearby your house and school and make people aware about healthy eating habits, not only this you must share the significance of saving this planet with them and motivate them to adopt habits which can help them in protecting the environment.

3. **Plan Your Act:** This can be conducted in groups of 4, students can create a planner wherein they need to mention all the steps they'll be taking to promote the goal Good Health and Well Being. They can also create their own targets which are essential to be achieved for the purpose of saving our dear Mother Earth and augmenting the eating habits of myriad individuals. These targets listed by them must be worked upon with immense vigour and group with the best outcome must be awarded by the teachers.

4. **Vaccination and Blood Donation Campaign:** With the help of your school leader and teachers you can organise a vaccination and blood donation camp in your school in order to promote good health. If possible then invite the parents or people living near your school to come and join this campaign.

5. **Time to Meditate:** Students can organise regular sessions for meditation in order to attain a healthy mind, body and spirit.

6. **Medication Box:** Students can create a box of different medicines and go to a rural area nearby the school premises in order to donate these medicines to those people who cannot afford to buy them. With the help of your teachers novices can conduct a free health check - up camp in such areas so that the best of health advice can be given to these people.

7. **Presentation on Global Risks:** A presentation can be created in order to enhance the awareness pertaining to various global issues that affect our health and well being, it must be really effective and penetrate the mind of various individuals with thoughts of acquiring and promoting the goal Good Health and Well Being.

8. **Non - Fire Cooking:** Students with the help of teachers can prepare some healthy snacks and share it with their peers and everybody else in the school in order to promote healthy eating habits. They can share recipes and talk about the benefits of inculcating such snacks in their regular diet.

SUSTAINABLE DEVELOPMENT GOALS

17 GOALS TO TRANSFORM OUR WORLD

#SDGSketch

is a project by @Club17Africa http://club17africa.org in collaboration with @lonirex and @DrMinaOgbanga

GOAL 4: Ensure inclusive and equitable quality education and promote lifelong learning opportunities for all

By 2030

All girls and boys complete free and quality primary and secondary education

Build and Upgrade education facilities child, disabilities and gender sensitive

All girls and boys access pre-primary education

Access to tertiary education for all men and women

Expand globally the number of scholarship available in Developing Countries

More Youths and Adults with relevant skills

Eliminate Gender Disparity in education

All learners acquire knowledge and skills to promote sustainable development among others

All Youths and a substential proportion of Adults achieve literacy and numeracy

More qualified Teachers specially in Developing Countries

GOAL 4: QUALITY EDUCATION

This goal promotes the fact that every individual despite of his caste, colour, creed, religion has the right of attaining a quality education. It opens doors of numerous opportunities for individuals so that they can strive hard towards their dreams and achieve them in an utmost manner, and hence is considered to be the key for prosperity. Those who'll work towards this goal will actually make a mark in the society and contribute in it being more progressive and healthy, however, what needs to be taken care of is the learning opportunities, they must be provided to all. There are many children in the world who are starving for education, hence it is essential for us to start acting towards it.

A good quality education provides virtuous learning opportunities to the learners so that they can take care of their economic needs, develop sustainable livelihoods and create a much desired well being for, they can not only contribute to the growth of their family but also work towards the development of their society and country. Therefore, there are few things which must be taken care of:

1. **Equity in Education:** Every child despite of his caste, colour and status must be given an equal right and opportunity to be educated, and no obstacle should block him/her to attain this.

2. **Extracting the best out of individual:** Education can never be of a supreme quality till the time it is delivered with love and passion so that the best can be extracted from each pupil. The focus must be on the overall development of a child.

3. **Balanced Approach:** Each child must be educated not just to become a proficient professional but even a responsible citizen of the country so that he can contribute in creating a democratic and peaceful society.

4. **Accomplishing Learning Outcomes:** Children must develop a certain level of understanding and skills after being educated which can only be achieved once the learning outcomes are accomplished in an utmost manner.

   A. **The significance of Quality Education:** Quality education is required because the world needs people who can play their role efficiently and contribute in the sustainability and development of this planet and its residents. Not only this, it is much needed for individuals to develop an appropriate skill set which can help them in earning a good income and enjoying a healthy well being. Apart from these reasons, there are certain other attributes which reflect upon the significance of goal 'Quality Education':

   B. **Foundation of a good life:** By working on this particular goal we can not only augment our life but also encourage people to build an amazing life for themselves.

   C. **Stable income:** It can enable pupils to prepare themselves for the competitive world and will enable them to face various challenges in the finest manner. This will also help them to acquire appropriate career opportunities and build a good source of income.

   D. **Equal Opportunities:** Quality Education can eliminate the differences between numerous social classes and genders. This particular goal holds a potential to make this world a just and fair place wherein every person is given an equal opportunity so that even poor people can get a chance to earn a decent income.

   E. **Achievement of dreams:** Education if delivered in an unsurpassed manner can help individuals to achieve their dreams as it will then provide will all the necessary aids which can turn them into proficient professionals and wonderful human beings.

   F. **Peace and Safety:** This goal ushers people to understand the difference between right and wrong, legal and illegal actions and so on which can make this world a peaceful and safe place for everybody. Also, an efficient education can enable people to be aware of their rights and duties towards the society which is imperative for the growth of any country.

4.2 Targets of the goal 'Quality Education':

Following are the targets of this particular goal which are expected to be achieved by 2030:

1. All the boys and girls must be given equal opportunities to attain early childcare education so that can be ready to attain the primary education later.

2. The learning outcomes must be accomplished efficiently so that the best can be extracted from all the pupils.

3. To enable youth and adults attain appropriate vocational and technical skills so that can utilise them to earn a good income.

4. Quality education must encourage individuals to appreciate gender equality, sustainable development, cultural diversity etc.

5. The number of qualified teachers must be increased so that they can deliver the best of education to all the novices.

4.3 How to accomplish Quality Education?

Following are the ways by which quality of education can be enhanced:

1. **Quality of the Content:** The content of curriculum must be effective, interesting and easy to understand so that students can comprehend it in the best possible manner.

2. **Effective Teaching Pedagogies:** The best of innovative methods must be used by teachers so that they can deliver the lesson effectively and attain various learning outcomes.

3. **Delivering the Lesson using Technologies:** Myriad technologies can be used by educators so that students can enjoy learning various skills and topics.

4. **Individual Attention:** Teachers must be aware of the strengths and weakness of all the students so that they can work on them accordingly. Special attention must be given to the ones who need it the most.

5. Success of the goal 'Quality Education' is a two-way process and doesn't depend upon teachers only, students also need to understand their role and responsibilities about the same so that a much-desired outcome can be attained:

6. **Prioritising the goals:** You as a student must prioritise your goals and work on each one of them accordingly.

7. **Work on academics:** Each lesson taught in the class must be taken seriously and the major emphasis of all the students must be on academics, this doesn't mean that they cannot participate in co-curricular activities but rather encourages equal participation and seriousness towards studies.

8. **Regular Attendance:** Novices must attend the classes regularly so that they do not miss out on important lessons and can be on the same page with teachers as well as their peers.

9. **Self – Discipline:** This is one of the most imperative goals for students, they must be disciplined and obedient. Teachers and parents are the best guides for them hence they must listen to them and follow their guidance persistently.

These are some of the goals for students, there are many other which can be explained by teachers with the help of different resources.

4.4: Student's involvement in promoting the goal 'Quality Education':

Here are few of the activities which students can conduct with the help of their teachers in order to encourage people to work towards the goal 'Quality Education':

1. **Educate a child:** Students can conduct Charity Camps on regular basis in the school or nearby areas and donate the amount collected to an organisation supporting the cause of educating the underprivileged kids.

2. **Books Donation:** Teachers can encourage children by donating their used school books to those who need them the most so that they can get virtuous learning opportunities.

3. **School Supply Survey:** Novices can conduct a survey in the surrounding areas of their school asking people about different supplies needed by them pertaining to their child's education. Based on the answers and with the help of teachers, principal, and management these supplies can be arranged and delivered to all such people.

4. **Buddy Up:** Junior students can be given an opportunity to be mentored by senior students on a regular basis so that they can augment themselves in different subjects and areas. Teachers can also take help from various students in improving those who lack an understanding of any topic or skill set.

5. **Field Trips:** Various field trips must be conducted by the school in order to make students get familiar with the culture of different countries this will help them enhance their knowledge and become influential.

6. **Learn with Experience:** Real life examples along with congruent exposure must be provided to students to make them gain an appropriate understanding of various concepts.

SUSTAINABLE DEVELOPMENT **GOALS**

#SDGSketch

17 GOALS TO TRANSFORM OUR WORLD

is a project by @Club17Africa http://club17africa.org in collaboration with @xLontrex and @DrMinaOgbanga

GOAL 5: Achieve gender equality and empower all women and girls

End all forms of discrimination against all Women and Girls

Undertake reforms to give Women equal rights to Economic Resources

Eliminate all forms of Violence against all Women and Girls

Ensure the use of enabling technology to promote the Empowerment of Women

Eliminate all Harmful Practices

Ensure Women's full and effective participation and equal opportunities for Leadership at all levels of Decision Making

Adopt and Strengthen sound policies and enforce legislation for the promotion of Gender Equality

Recognize and Value Unpaid Care and Domestic Work

Ensure universal access to sexual and reproductive health and reproductive rights

GOAL 5: GENDER EQUALITY

Gender equality, equality between men and women, entails the concept that all human beings, both men and women are free to develop their personal abilities and make choices without the limitations set by stereotypes, rigid gender roles and prejudices. Gender equality means that the different behaviour, aspirations, and needs of women and men are considered, valued and favoured equally. It doesn't mean that women and men have to become the same, but that their rights, responsibilities and opportunities will not depend on whether they are born male or female. Gender equity means fairness of treatment for women and men, according to their respective needs. This may include equal treatment or treatment that is different but which is considered equivalent in terms of rights, benefits, obligations and opportunities.

— ABC Of Women Worker's Rights And Gender Equality, ILO, 2000. p. 48.

The inequality between genders is not only a social issue but a problem which is destroying our society and creating a waste of the human potential. By not allowing women to live according to their rights we are denying half of our worldly population to live a life according to their wish, we must understand that the growth of any country can immensely enhance once equal opportunities are given to both the genders.

This is the purpose of the goal 'Gender Equality', to eliminate any sort of discrimination between genders and allowing both, men and women to get equal opportunities in the social, economic and political world.

Not only this, the goal 'Gender Equality' aim towards the accomplishment of men and women enjoying the same rights, if we wish to successfully attain the achievement of sustainable development goals then this particular one is the most crucial one. One of the guiding principles of the 2030 Agenda for Development states that 'We must not leave anyone behind' and hence. if we wish to see this world as a wonderful home for all then its imperative for all to work towards this goal.

5.1 The significance of goal Gender Equality:

A. This goal work towards women empowerment and hence encourages people to act congruently.

B. Once women will be provided with equal rights and opportunities they can then serve in building a healthy, successful and prosperous nation.

5.2 Targets of the goal 'Gender Equality':

No goal can be achieved unless and until we act towards it, so in order to eliminate inequality among genders here are few of the targets which we must take seriously and work upon with an utmost vigour:

A. **Say 'No' to discrimination:** Women needs to be respected the same as men and must be given equal rights and opportunities and all sort of discrimination must be eliminated.

B. **End of violence and exploitation against women and girls:** All kind of violence and exploitation against men and women must be ended. Appropriate measures must be taken to protect them against trafficking, child labor, and congruent exploitations.

C. **Forced marriages must be abolished:** There must be an end put up on forced or child marriages and both and children must be encouraged to get educated and build an astounding career.

D. **Leadership Opportunities:** Equal leadership opportunities must be given to men and women, and both should be involved in all levels of decision making in social, political and economic life.

E. **Equal Rights and Opportunities:** Women should be given equal rights in property as well as other economic resources.

F. **Empowerment through technology:** Opportunities must be provided to women in order to make themselves aware of different technologies so that they augment themselves in the desired areas.

5.3. How to accomplish Gender Equality?

Let's look in a little detail how can this particular goal be achieved successfully:

A. **Creating awareness:** Girls and women need to be explained about the significance of education, not only this they must be given counselling sessions so that they can realise their potential and use it appropriately instead of wasting it.

B. **Empowering Mothers:** Mothers need to be counselled and given appropriate parenting sessions, she should be explained the significance of educating a girl child, all the information must be given to the mothers which can help them in bringing up their daughters in an utmost manner.

5.4 Student's involvement in promoting the goal 'Gender Equality':

Here are few of the activities which students can conduct with the help of their teachers in order to encourage their peers and other people to support the goal ' Gender Equality':

A. **Voice your support:** Students must raise their voice and create awareness around this goal, they must also raise a point that men and women must be paid equally and without any discrimination. They can be very creative about this campaign and make it very effective with the valuable guidance and support of their leaders and mentors.

B. **Harassment Forum:** Novices with the help of their mentors can create a forum which can provide all the necessary support against any sort of harassment, this forum must be created for the students as well as educators in the school campus. Students must create various guidelines and policies related to the same and must select the council members which may include children as well as teachers.

C. **Mentorship Program:** Students can speak to various organisations that are working towards this particular goal and arrange a mentorship program for their fellow mates, this can encompass visits, workshops or anything else which can encourage their peers to work towards this particular goal.

D. **Awareness Drive:** Regular sessions must be conducted in the school premises which can not only enhance the knowledge of students but even make teachers more aware of this particular goal.

SUSTAINABLE DEVELOPMENT **GOALS**

17 GOALS TO TRANSFORM OUR WORLD

#SDGSketch

is a project by @Club17Africa http://club17africa.org in collaboration with @xlemtrex and @DrMinaOgbanga

GOAL6: Ensure availability and sustainable management of water and sanitation for all

By 2030

Universal and equitable access to drinking water for all

Adequate and equitable sanitation and hygiene for all

By 2020 protect and restore Water Related Ecosystems

Expand International cooperation and capacity-building support to developing countries in water activities and programs

Improve water quality, increase recycling and safe reuse globally

Implement integrated Water Resource Management

Support and strengthen the participation of local communities in improving water and sanitation management

GOAL 6 : CLEAN WATER AND SANITATION

Out of every three people, there is one who stays without proper sanitation which results in poor health and sometimes even death. Many drives and activities were conducted in the past in order to promote the significance of clean water and sanitation, however, the major reason for the failure of such initiatives and drives was lack of essential equipments. If you look at the exact statistics then you'll be shocked to know that only two and a half billion people have access to healthy drinking water and congruent sources on a global level since 1990 and there are approximately six hundred and sixty - three people who are still living without clean water and proper sanitation facilities. Not only this, almost 1000 children die each day due to numerous preventable diseases, and the main reason for them being affected by such diseases is lack of clean water and sanitation.

Access to clean water is absolutely crucial if we want to live a healthy life, our planet has good and sufficient water which if used judiciously can be provided to every person. The Sustainable Development Goals have helped myriad international communities and corporations in resolving the problems related to water and sanitation by enabling them to conduct various activities and programs related to the same. Improving sanitation is a key and priority for every government and hence they run many flagship programs which can help them encourage people to work towards this particular goal. Namami Gange, Swacch Bharat Abhiyan, National Rural Drinking Water are few of the programs conducted in India to promote the significance of goal 'Clean Water and Sanitation'.

6.1 Significance of the goal 'Clean Water and Sanitation':

1.   Water plays an imperative part in the nutrition of an individual, hence clean water will always help one to stay healthy.

2.   Lack of water at public toilets, schools, malls, clinics etc create problems for women especially during their menstrual cycle, hence we need clean water at such places so that they can stay hygienic and healthy.

3.   The access to clean water can help us in staying away from various diseases like stomach infections, diarrhoea etc.

Hence with the help of this particular goal, we can improve the condition of water and sanitation in our society and make this world a safe and healthy home for all.

6.2. Targets of the goal 'Clean Water and Sanitation':

Below mentioned are the targets of this particular goal which are expected to be achieved by the year 2030:

1.   By 2030, there must be access to safe and affordable drinking water on a global level.

2.   An end must be put to open defecation and special attention must be paid to the hygiene of women and girls especially the ones in vulnerable conditions.

3.   The quality of water must be enhanced by working on the reduction of pollution and minimising dumping of hazardous chemicals. Not only this, there must be enough focus given to recycling and safe re-use on a global level.

4.   By 2030, the issue of water scarcity and quality must be eliminated in the best possible manner.

5. There are a good number of organisations who are working towards the goal 'Clean Water and Sanitation'. Enough support must be provided to them so that they can accomplish their targets easily.

6.3. Accomplishing the goal 'Clean Water and Sanitation':

There are various problems related to water and sanitation which are affecting this entire planet adversely and hence must be taken care of as soon as possible. Here are few of the things which can help in flipping the coin over and enhancing the situation of those who are suffering from a lack of proper water and sanitation facilities:

1. Planning expenditure on the development of the water sector.

2. Improving the conservation and management of water resources.

3. Making the sanitation facilities really effective.

4. Strengthening municipal responsibility and ownership in water supply and sanitation.

5. Well managed communal facilities must be arranged for high – density urban areas.

6. The accountability of providers must be enhanced.

7. Hygiene awareness must be created as much as possible.

8. All the activities which result in water pollution must be stopped.

6.4. Student's involvement in the goal 'Clean Water and Sanitation':

Students with the help of their mentors can conduct the following activities to promote the significance of 'Clean Water and Sanitation' in their campus as well as surrounding areas:

1. The students must create a map of all the places in their school where they can find clean water. Once these places are marked, they need to go and check whether their observation about those places was apt or not. If not, they would need to create an action plan on how they can turn things around and share this plan with their teachers and mentors.

2. The students must be taken out and instructed to find sources of clean water which must not be easily available for them. Once they complete this activity, they must be explained how many people do this on a daily basis, and what is the significance of drinking clean water.

3. Teachers must apply glitter on the hands of students and ask them to wash it with the normal water without using soap when the children fail to wash off the glitter ask them to wash their hands with soap water. This is one the best techniques to explain children about the significance of clean water.

4. Conduct a survey in your school wherein each student will be required to monitor the water usage at their home. Do this for a week and then discuss it in the class. It will then be easy for the novices to understand the need for saving water.

5. The students with the help of their mentors can organise a cleanup project wherein they will be expected to clean a local river, seaside etc. They can create a report or blog on it and share it on the social media in order to enhance the awareness of other people.

6. There are more than 4 million people who refrain themselves from getting proper sanitation facilities. Raise your voice on various platforms for this particular issue and ensure it reaches to a good number of people.

SUSTAINABLE DEVELOPMENT **GOALS**   #SDGSketch

17 GOALS TO TRANSFORM OUR WORLD

is a project by @Club17Africa http://club17africa.org in collaboration with @xlontrex and @DrMinaOgbanga

GOAL 7: Ensure access to affordable, reliable, sustainable and modern energy for all

By 2030

Double the global rate of improvement in energy efficiency

Substantially increase the share of renewable energy in the energy mix

Expand infrastructure and upgrade technology for supplying modern and sustainable energy services for all in developing countries

Universal access to affordable, reliable and modern energy services

Enhance international cooperation to facilitate access to clean energy research and technology

GOAL 7: AFFORDABLE AND CLEAN ENERGY

People who aren't given sustainable access to energy cannot be a part of national or global progress. You will be amazed to know that there are around one billion people across the globe who are deprived of access to energy. Not only this, three billion people around the world aren't given access to clean fuel and technologies which can be used in effective cooking.

1.   Sustainable energy generates a lot of opportunities and can enable people to transform their lives, economies as well as this planet. The production of energy is also responsible for the changes that are taking place in the climate these days, tangible energy is responsible for the health and well being of individuals and is also a reason for the augmentation of the same. Without energy, it is not possible for people to study, travel, take up jobs , start a business etc. It is responsible for the climatic changes, food production and various opportunities that can enhance one's income.

2.   The secretary of United Nations, Ban Ki – moon has shared this empowering thought about energy "Energy is the golden thread that connects economic growth, social equity, and environmental sustainability. The production of usable energy can also be a source of climate change – accounting for around 60 % of total global greenhouse gas emissions." The goal of affordable and clean energy is to develop a sustainable energy for all and providing a universal access to efficient, clean and reliable sources and services of energy.

7.1 The significance of Affordable and Clean Energy:

1. Clean energy can reduce leaving a harmful effect on the environment.

2. It can reduce harmful smog, and impacts caused by coal mining and gas extraction.

3. The renewable energy source can be utilised to produce electricity without impacting the environment adversely.

4. It can conserve the natural resources of a particular nation.

5. For all these and many other reasons, this particular goal has been created and myriad efforts are being put in so that these and all the other targets can be achieved.

7.2. Targets of the goal 'Affordable and Clean Energy':

Below mentioned are the targets which are expected to be achieved by 2030 for the accomplishment of this particular goal:

1. **Global access to modern energy:** To ensure that universal access to affordable as well as reliable modern energy services must be provided to all.

2. **Enhancement of energy efficiency:** By 2030, the efficiency of energy must be doubled so that the best results can be attained.

3. **Expanding energy services for underdeveloped countries:** The best energy services must be provided to the developing countries.

4. **Research and Development:** By 2030 effective methods must be designed with the help of an effective research process to enhance the quality of energy.

7.3. Accomplishing the goal 'Affordable and Clean Energy':

This particular goal can be accomplished by working on some of the green alternative energy tips

1. **Switching to green power:** This can be done by getting in touch with the current provider and figure out if they can offer some alternative solutions which can enhance the quality of energy in different homes and areas.

2. **Using Solar Power:** There's two type of solar power, active and passive. Active solar power is used by capturing solar cells and can be stored to be used later or even immediately to provide heat or electricity. Passive power can act as power grids and can be used in getting power at night or during turbulent weather. It is the one which uses power of the sun to heat your home and can keep an area heated during winter and cool in the summer season.

3. **Wind energy:** Wind energy is considered to be the cleanest form of energies hence using wind turbines is one of the appropriate ways of cleaning the energy.

4. Apart from these, there are numerous other ways which can clean the energy and is quite affordable. So use different resources and figure out more of such innovative methods which can help in the accomplishment of this goal.

7.4. Student's involvement in the goal 'Affordable and Clean Energy':

Students can do a lot of research work and figure out methods which can help them in working towards this goal. Apart from that there are few activities they can try their hands on in order to accomplish the targets pertaining to this particular goal:

1. **Saving the energy:** Students must develop this habit and encourage their peers to switch off all the lights and the necessary equipments when not in use. Create awareness about

    this goal and motivate people to reduce the use of air conditioners and open windows to get fresh air.

2. **School campaign:** Run a campaign in your school wherein you'll create awareness among students and teachers to use rechargeable electronics instead of one – use batteries. Not only this, share the importance of solar technology with them and encourage them to use it.

SUSTAINABLE DEVELOPMENT GOALS

17 GOALS TO TRANSFORM OUR WORLD

#SDGSketch

is a project by @Club17Africa http://club17africa.org in collaboration with @Lantrex and @DrMinaOgbanga

GOAL 8: Promote sustained, inclusive and sustainable economic growth, full and productive employment and decent work for all

7%

Sustain per capita economic growth in particular, at least 7% gross domestic product/year in least developed Countries

Achieve higher level of economic productivity through Diversification, Technological upgrading, and Innovation

Protect labour rights and

Eradicate promote safe and forced labour, secure working modern slavery environment and human trafficking

Improve global resource efficiency in consumption and production to decouple economic growth from environmental degradation

Promote Sustainable Tourism

Strengthen the capacity of Domestic Financial Institutions

Promote development-oriented Policies and encourage the formalization and growth of micro-small and medium-sized Enterprises

By 2030 achieve

full productive employment for all women, men, young people and person with disabilities

AID for TRADE

Increase Aid for Trade support in Developing Countries

By 2020 reduce the proportion of youth NOT in employment, education or training

ILO By 2020

develop and operationalize a global strategy for youth employment and implement the Global Job Pact of the Int'l Labour Org.

GOAL 8: DECENT WORK AND ECONOMIC GROWTH

Economic growth is immensely essential for the growth of any country, hence we must ensure that enormous job opportunities are created without harming the environment so that it can be accomplished in the best possible manner. It is imperative to protect the labor rights and appropriate actions must be taken against child labor as the purpose of this goal is to ensure that this planet experiences the desired economic growth so that the people living here can live a good life.

The statistics reflect that the unemployment has increased from 170 million in 2007 to approximately 202 million in the year 2012, the lack of decent work opportunities has affected the world economy on an enormous level. In the year 2012, around 82 million children over the world were involved in many unsafe jobs, therefore this particular goal was created so that all the undesired causes that are affecting the world economy could be eliminated. Decent economic growth can make this world really prosperous and stronger economies can create more opportunities to build a sustainable world. Such a growth is not restricted to monetary success only, but also focusses on the well being of all, especially the ones who are treated with inequality, unfair means and are vulnerable because of this. If we look at the mission statement of global goals which states 'No one left behind' reflects on the significance of working for the welfare of all and this is the beauty of the goal 'Decent work and economic growth' which ensures the well being on a global level by 2030 if worked upon in an utmost manner. It is estimated that the world would require approximately 470 million jobs worldwide and hence necessary steps must be taken for the accomplishment of this particular goal.

8.1. The significance of goal 'Decent Work and Economic Growth':

Following points indicate the significance of goal 'Decent Work and Economic Growth':

1. Economic growth is essential to improve the standard of living.

2. This particular goal can enhance the GDP of the society instead of population.

3. It can meet new standards and resolve various social and economic problems.

4. Economic growth is important for job creations.

5. It can improve the quality of life.

8.2. Targets of the goal 'Decent Work and Economic Growth':

Below mentioned are the targets which must be worked upon in order to ensure that this goal is accomplished in the best possible manner:

1. **Obtaining a sustainable economic growth:** There must be a sustainability in the per capita income in congruence with the national circumstances.

2. **Innovation in economic productivity:** An enhanced economic productivity can be attained with the help of various technological upgradation.

3. **Policies must be created for job creation:** Development - oriented policies must be promoted so that good number of jobs can be created, not only this, financial access must be provided to small and medium- sized enterprises so that they can grow and flourish appropriately.

4. **Equal pay opportunities:** Equal growth opportunities must be provided to men and women and equal pay must be given for the equal value of work.

5. **Sustainable Tourism:** By the year 2030, suitable policies must be created and implemented pertaining to sustainable tourism so that myriad job opportunities can be created and traditional products can be promoted.

6. **Desired access to banking and financial services:** The capacity of domestic financial institutions must be strengthened so that the access to financial and insurance services can be increased.

7. **Global youth employment strategy:** Global strategy must be created for youth employment and implemented appropriately in order to enhance the economic growth on a global level.

8.3. Accomplishing the target 'Decent Work and Economic Growth':

Following points must be considered to enhance the economic growth of any country:

1. **Enhancing economic growth with innovative methods:** Various innovative methods must be created to enhance the skill sets of individuals so that it becomes easy for them to get into good jobs or start up virtuous businesses.

2. **People must be encouraged to come out of unemployment:** In many countries the citizens get a decent amount of income in case they are out of jobs, this encourages some of them to stay unemployed, such sort of people must be motivated to take up jobs and not to stay dependent on the government for money.

3. **Green cards must be given to capable people:** Various companies in the world need immensely capable people who can take their business up to an exalted levels of success, such people must be given citizenship of the desired countries because they are the ones who can strive hard to boost the economy there and work towards the welfare of other people.

4. **Introduction of new management techniques:** Better relationships at work can help in the productivity of employees hence congruent policies must be developed which can work out for the welfare of both the employer, as well as employee. Enhanced productivity can result in the growth of organisations and augment the economy in the best possible manner.

5. **Retirement age should be raised:** Once this is done there will be chances of efficient people working for a longer period and this will also affect the economy of a particular country in an unsurpassed manner.

8.4. Student's involvement in promoting the goal of 'Decent Work and Economic Growth':

Students with the help of their teachers or mentors can conduct the following activities in order to promote the goal of 'Decent Work and Economic Growth':

1. **Mentoring Program:** Get in touch with proficient and recognised organisations in your area and try and arrange a summit in your campus wherein eminent speakers from these organisations can come over and share their experience and knowledge with all the students which can enhance their knowledge on becoming virtuous and capable professionals in the future.

2. **Raise your voice:** Students can conduct a rally or street show to showcase the importance of using original products instead of buying cheap ones. Not only this, people must be encouraged to buy goods and products from the local producers only.

3. **Read and Share:** This can be done as a group activity wherein each group needs to collect information about renowned people involved in various business practices and present it in front of their peers in the form of a presentation.

SUSTAINABLE DEVELOPMENT **GOALS** #SDGSketch

17 GOALS TO TRANSFORM OUR WORLD

is a project by @Club17Africa http://club17africa.org in collaboration with @xlentrex and @DrMinaOgbanga

GOAL 9: Build resilient infrastructure, promote inclusive and sustainable industrialization and foster innovation

Develop quality, reliable, sustainable and resilient Infrastructure

Increase the access of small-scale industries and other enterprises to financial services

Enhance scientific research and technology, particularly in developing countries and, by 2030, encourage innovation

By 2030 raise industry's share of employment and GDP

Update infrastructures and retrofit industries to make them sustainable

Facilitate sustainable and resilient infrastructure development in developing countries and small island developing States

Support domestic technology development, research and innovation in developing countries

Increase access to information and communication technologies to provide access to Internet

GOAL 9: INDUSTRY, INNOVATION, AND INFRASTRUCTURE

The infrastructure of our industries must be enhanced so that they can be well prepared to meet various challenges that are blocking their expansion and growth. The best way to attain this goal is to work towards innovation, new technologies must be discovered so that it can impact these industries in an appropriate way and help in generating good products and business. Universal access must be provided to the desired information and financial markets as this will help in bringing in prosperity, increasing job opportunities, and building affluent cities across the globe.

Appropriate investment is required in order to enhance the condition of industries and bringing in different innovational technologies, in fact, it is the driving force behind the economic growth and development of any country. The population living in developed cities and countries is increasing day by day which increases the significance of mass transport and renewable energy, sustainable industries cannot be created without investing in scientific research and innovation which are the essential steps towards sustainable development.

There are four billion people across the globe who don't have access to the internet and you'll be amazed to know that ninety percent of them are from developing cities and countries. It is essential for us to bridge this gap if we wish to achieve this particular goal, a lot of brainstorming, planning and above all execution is required for its accomplishment, but if done properly it can bring a great difference in the economy as well as the welfare of countries on a global level.

9.1.The significance of goal 'Industry, Innovation and Infrastructure':

Following points reflect upon the importance of this particular goal:

1. Investment in innovation and technology are essential for the economic development of various cities and countries.

2. Promoting this goal will enhance the chances of accomplishing sustainable development by the year 2030.

3. Technological progress is one of the best solutions to deal with economic as well as environmental challenges.

4. This goal will enhance various job opportunities which will certainly impact the economy of any city or country in an effective and positive manner.

9.2. Targets of the goal 'Industry, Innovation and Infrastructure':

Below mentioned are the targets which must be achieved in order to achieve this goal in the best possible manner, each target is crucial and important and must be worked upon seriously and appropriately. These targets are responsible for building efficient infrastructure, fostering innovation and promoting sustainable industrialisation:

1. **Developing quality infrastructure:** Quality infrastructure must be created in order to support the economic development and well – being while being aware of its inexpensive and equal access for all. The infrastructure must be upgraded keeping the sustainability of virtuous environment in mind.

2. **Promoting Sustainable Industrialisation:** Immense focus must be put on achieving sustainable industrialisation, not only this the ratio of employment and gross domestic product must be enhanced up to a decent extent, which means that it should be doubled in the developing countries.

3. **Increased access to financial services:** Affordable loans or credits must be provided to the small - scale industries existing in

different developing countries and they should be given an appropriate access to different financial services which can enable them to grow in an utmost manner.

4. **Enhancing Scientific Research and Technology Upgradation:** Effective scientific research must be conducted in a way that can upgrade the technological capabilities of various organisations and industries in the developing countries. Numerous innovative methods must be figured out which can prove out to be beneficial for the economic as well as environmental growth of different cities and countries.

5. **Universal access to information and technology:** Universal access to internet and congruent facilities must be provided on a global level by the year 2030.

9.3. Accomplishing the goal ' Industry, Innovation and Infrastructure':

Below mentioned are the points which if worked upon efficiently can result in the achievement of this goal:

1. **Strengthening the economy:** Once the economy of a city or country will reach up to an enormous state the improvement in infrastructure can be easily created.

2. **Improving the utilisation of infrastructure:** The appropriate utilisation of infrastructure will help in the achievement of this goal.

3. **An Investment must be made in idea generation:** Best of innovative practices must be created with a decent amount of investment so that myriad technologies can be upgraded and opportunities must be created for the purpose of economic growth of various cities and countries.

4. **Use additional resources for innovation:** Different resources must be found and used so that innovation can take place in the

best possible manner. It is not a one-step solution and needs numerous attributes in order to be successful.

9.4. Student's involvement in promoting the goal ' Industry, Innovation and Infrastructure':

Students with the help of their teachers or mentors need to promote the significance of this goal by conducting the following activities:

1. **Thinking out of the box:** This is a group activity wherein each group is given a topic and students must be encouraged to brainstorm and come out with some realistic and innovative solutions for the same. Novices can also prepare models and congruent solutions in order to promote the significance of their chosen topic and the possible exhibition on this can be a great idea.

2. **Kill the stupid rules:** This is an amazing game to enable critical thinking, create two teams and give them ten mins to answer the question 'Which stupid rules would you like to kill, how and what would you replace them with?". Look forward to some wonderful and innovative answers.

3. **Brain teasers and puzzles:** Conduct quizzes, ask your fellow students to solve some of the most interesting brain teasers and puzzles in order to juggle their brain and make it more innovative.

4. **Think Tank:** Create a questionnaire to check the knowledge of your peers and help them juggle their brain to find solutions for the hindrances related to this particular goal.

SUSTAINABLE DEVELOPMENT GOALS

17 GOALS TO TRANSFORM OUR WORLD

#SDGSketch

is a project by @Club17Africa http://club17africa.org in collaboration with @xLenirax and @DrMinaOgbanga

GOAL 10: Reduce inequality within and among countries

By 2030 achieve and sustain income growth of the bottom 40% of the population

Improve regulation and monitoring of global financial markets and institutions

Facilitate orderly, safe, regular and responsible migration and mobility of people

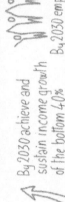

By 2030 empower and promote the social, political and economic inclusion for all

Ensure enhanced representation and voice for developing countries in decision making in global international and financial institutions

Implement the principle of special and differential treatment for developing countries

Eliminate discriminatory laws, policies and practices

Adopt policies, especially fiscal, wage and social protection policies to progressively achieve greater equality

Encourage official development assistance and financial flow to States where the need is greatest

By 2030 reduce to less than 3% the transaction cost for migrant remittances

GOAL 10: REDUCED INEQUALITY

This goal talks about the inequality of income which is taking place in many countries and is one of the most crucial problems which needs a global solution. This can be done once the monitoring will start happening around various financial institutions and markets. You'll be surprised to know that the poorest 10 percent of the population of this world earn only 2 or 7 percent of the total global income. As the population is on a rise, with it the problem of inequality is also increasing, in fact, it has increased up to 11 percent if we look at it worldwide. As this problem exists globally, therefore it needs solutions on the global level, one of the solutions can be to work upon the goal 'Reducing Inequalities' which can help in the elimination of this problem that leads to financial and social discrimination.

In case nations feel the need of experiencing a virtuous economy and expect its people to flourish then equality of income can play a major role in achieving this. There must be equality amongst individuals regardless of their colour, caste, creed, religious beliefs, economic status etc. The individuals must be encouraged and given an opportunity to be self-sufficient and once this will be done, it will then become easier for us to accomplish this goal efficiently.

10.1 Significance of the goal 'Reduced Inequality':

Following are the points which reflect upon the significance of this goal:

1. This goal promotes the significance of equality among individuals who are living together in the same city or country.

2. As this goal supports the cause of women getting equal financial benefits and rights, it can enhance global income fantastically.

3. Once their come will get appropriate and stable there will be higher chances of economies to get sustainable, equal societies promote equal growth opportunities for all which also brings in prosperity and help people work towards their common good.

10.2 Targets of the goal 'Reduced Inequality'

Below mentioned are the targets which must be achieved in order to achieve this goal in the best possible manner, each target is crucial and important and must be worked upon seriously and appropriately. These targets are responsible for bringing in more stability and equality in the income of various individuals despite of their caste, creed and colour:

1. By the year 2030, all those laws, policies and practices which cause discrimination in the society must be eliminated.

2. All those policies which promote equality must be adopted by various countries worldwide as this will help them to succeed and flourish easily.

3. The monitoring and regulation of various institutions and financial markets must be done on a regular basis and appropriate regulations must be strengthened.

4. Responsible and safe migration facilities must be provided to people so that their mobility can become easy and effective which can be done by implementing apt migration policies.

These are some of the targets, there are multiple other targets which can help in the accomplishment of this goal.

10.3 Accomplishment of the goal 'Reduced Inequalities':

Following measures can be taken in order to accomplish the goal 'Reduced Inequalities':, in fact there few of the proficient policies which must be worked upon in order to eliminate the problem of inequality:

1. Regular increments must be done in the wages of people on the timely basis, one of the researches show that the increase in the wages of low paid workers can enable near about 4.6 million people to come out of the poverty.

2. Different policies must be formed which can enable people from different family backgrounds to enhance their income and savings. Such policies must be created that can give an opportunity to the middle-class families to attain a decent economic security for their family.

3. Education is one asset which neither be robbed nor lost, hence desired investments must be made by people in order to educate their children so that they can become independent and responsible citizens of the country.

Apart from them, there are many other measures which can be taken in order to achieve this goal successfully, all you need to do is to involve yourself in some research based activities and find out more about this.

10.4 Student's involvement in the goal 'Reduced Inequalities':

Students with the help of their teachers or mentors can promote the significance of this goal by conducting the following activities:

1. **Charity Camp:** Conduct a charity camp in your school on a quarterly basis and donate the money to an organisation which is working towards the development of people and society. Remember any donation, big or small can make a huge difference!

2. **Form a committee:** You need to form a school/student committee who can fight against any sort of inequality taking place within or outside your school campus.

3. **Time to Vote:** Help your peers in getting into a habit of collecting votes before choosing anyone as a monitor, prefect, captain and so on.

4. **Refugee Camp:** Conduct a Refugee Camp in your school or nearby areas and collect various materials and things which can help the migrants and refugees in your area or community.

SUSTAINABLE DEVELOPMENT **GOALS** #SDGSketch

17 GOALS TO TRANSFORM OUR WORLD

is a project by @Club17Africa http://club17africa.org in collaboration with @xLonirax and @DrMinaOgbanga

GOAL 11: Make cities and human settlements inclusive, safe, resilient and sustainable

By 2030 ensure access for all to adequate, safe and affordable housing

By 2030 reduce the number of death and people affected to economic losses caused by disasters

By 2030 provide access to safe, affordable, accessible and sustainable transport systems for all

Support positive economic, social and environmental links between urban, per-urban and rural areas

By 2030 reduce the averse per capita environmental impact of cities

By 2020 increase the number of cities adopting the SENDAI Framework for Disaster Risk Reduction

By 2030 enhance inclusive and sustainable urbanization and capacity for participatory, integrated and sustainable human settlements

Strengthen efforts to protect and safeguard the world's cultural and natural heritage

By 2030 provide universal access to safe, inclusive and accessible green and public spaces

Support least developed countries in building sustainable and resilient buildings with local materials

GOAL 11: SUSTAINABLE CITIES AND COMMUNITIES

The purpose of this goal is to make cities and human settlements safe, inclusive, sustainable and resilient. As we all are aware that the population of the world is increasing on a constant basis hence it is essential for us to think about the accommodation of our upcoming generation for which it is imperative to build sustainable and modern cities so that they don't face any problem in the future. Not only our next generation but even the existing one needs good facilities in order to enhance their standard of living and well being. For the purpose of living safely, and enjoying a prosperous life we need to make necessary amendments in the cities so that this goal can be attained without any hassles. This development would need virtuous urban planning, affordable cities with good and green environment along with culturally inspiring living conditions.

This or any other goal is difficult to achieve till the time proper actions are taken pertaining to them, people must be made aware about the modern style of living and advantages of the same must be explained to them so that it gives them a boost to work towards this particular goal.

Nearly more than half of the population is surviving in the urban areas and it is important that we understand that sustainable development cannot be attained unless and until we work towards the development of these areas. Poverty is increasing in these areas at present and it's getting difficult for the city and national governments to migrate new residents there. Affordable living is the need of the hour in these areas and must be attained if we really are expecting some good development there, for which the following attributes must be worked upon, affordable housing, a good investment in public transport, building green public spaces, enhancement in the urban planning and execution and so on.

11.1 Significance of the goal 'Sustainable Cities and Communities'

Following points can explain the significance or importance of this particular goal:

1. Sustainable Cities and Communities can make life easier for almost everybody living in a particular city or country.

2. The concept of affordable housing can enable people to get proper accommodations.

3. Once the transport system of any particular city or country will be developed, the condition of people living there will automatically enhance.

4. Resource efficient cities can combine wonderful output along with brilliant innovative methods and a combination of affordable prices for different consumers.

11.2 Targets of the goal ' Sustainable Cities and Communities'

Below mentioned are the targets which must be achieved in order to achieve this goal in the best possible manner, each target is crucial and important and must be worked upon seriously and appropriately. Once these targets will be worked upon efficiently there will be higher chances of augmentation in various cities and communities, and hence this makes the accomplishment of these targets extremely essential:

1. By 2030 proper housing facilities and basic services must be arranged for the residents as well as migrants from different cities and countries. Not only this, slums must be upgraded so that the entire nation can experience a better standard of living.

2. Transport must be made safe and easily accessible for all, not only this even the quality of roads must be improved. These changes must be made keeping in mind different

vulnerable situations of women, children and people with any sort of disability.

3.   **Protection of the world's natural heritage:** Stringent efforts must be put in for the purpose of making the cultural and natural heritage of the world sustainable.

4.   **Overcoming the loss caused by natural disasters:** Many people have lost their lives in different natural disasters that have occurred in the past, this needs to be worked upon so that the number does not increase in the future as the human loss is also responsible for the economic loss of a country or city.

5.   **Improving the environmental impact of cities**: Myriad effective measures must be taken in order to improve the air quality, waste management, and other municipal facilities.

6.   **Supporting least developed countries:** A helping hand must be provided to all those countries which are extremely underdeveloped. Till the time these countries will not be worked upon it will be difficult to achieve sustainable development on a global level.

These are a few of the targets and there are many other which must be worked upon effectively in order to accomplish this particular goal successfully.

11.3 Accomplishing the goal 'Sustainable Cities and Communities'

Following steps can be taken in order to make the cities and communities sustainable:

1.   The condition of slums and congruent areas must be improved and for this, all the necessary measures must be taken without fail. Even the urban cities need development these days hence proper plan must be laid out which can help

in the identification of challenges and ideas to overcome them.

2.   Effective programs which can contribute in the development and growth on a global level must be adopted and worked upon seriously.

3.   Individuals living in different cities and countries must be given enough opportunities to develop their skills so that they can contribute to the growth of the nation.

4.   Getting good accommodations must not be considered as a problem and people must be encouraged to offer some part of their house for the purpose of renting. This will solve the purpose of numerous migrants and will enable them to live safely and comfortably.

11.4 Students involvement in the goal 'Sustainable Cities and Communities:

Students with the help of their teachers or mentors need to promote the significance of this goal by conducting the following activities:

1.   Create a team of students and visit different slum areas, conduct workshops for the people there to make them familiarised with different methods that can help them in improving their living conditions. Click pictures and upload them on your school's website and social media in order to spread the word.

2.   Be a role model for your peers and encourage them to adopt sustainable ways of commuting like walking, cycling, and congruent activities.

3.   Inspire your fellow students, friends, and people living nearby your house to come forward and work towards in contributing to better public places, some of such activities may encompass trimming and watering of plants, renovating different areas etc.

These are few of the activities, students must be encouraged to involve themselves in research work and find out more of them so that this goal can be promoted and worked upon in the best possible manner.

SUSTAINABLE DEVELOPMENT **GOALS** #SDGSketch

17 GOALS TO TRANSFORM OUR WORLD

is a project by @Club17Africa http://club17africa.org in collaboration with @xlantrax and @DrMinaOgbanga

GOAL 12: Ensure sustainable consumption and production patterns

Implement the 10-year framework of programmes on sustainable consumption and production

By 2030 halve per capita food waste at the retail and consumer level

Promote sustainable public procurement practices

By 2030 ensure that people everywhere have the relevant information and awareness about sustainable development

By 2030 achieve the sustainable management and efficient use of natural resources

Encourage companies, especially large and transnational companies to adopt sustainable practices

Support developing countries to move toward more sustainable patterns of production and consumption

By 2020 achieve the environmentally sound management of chemicals and all wastes throughout their life cycle

By 2030 substantially reduce waste generation through prevention, reduction, recycling and reuse

Develop and implement tools to monitor development impacts for sustainable tourism

Rationalize inefficient fossil-fuel subsidies that encourage wasteful consumption

GOAL 12: RESPONSIBLE CONSUMPTION AND PRODUCTION

4. There are ample natural resources available on our planet but they are not utilised responsibly which as a result has caused harm to this planet. So the purpose of this goal is to how to produce as well as use these resources with immense responsibility so that they not only can be consumed properly, but even be utilised in the best possible manner and without being wasted, we really need to learn this in case we are willing to make this planet a sustainable home for all. Moreover, it is not only about producing and consuming the resources and energy efficiently, it is also about creating a sustainable infrastructure, working on the overall development, providing better facilities, creating good job opportunities, in short, the purpose of this and every other sustainable goal is to create a better quality of life.

5. In this current era when the need and consumption of natural resources is increasing, the environment is adversely affected by air, water, and soil pollution, not only these but there are many other factors which are not doing justice to the healthy sustainability of this planet. The focus must also be made on the supply chain wherein everyone from producer to the consumer is involved. This can only be done when an awareness around sustainable consumption and lifestyle will be created with the help of education, and all the essential information about the same is circulated among people.

12.1 Significance of the goal of 'Responsible Consumption and Production'

Following points can explain the significance or importance of this particular goal:

1. Natural resources have been important since ages for the purpose of successful development of countries.

2. These resources play the role of the most imperative driver of the economic development of nations and therefore must be taken care of properly.

3. Natural resources are also responsible for the technological development of countries and hence must be maintained appropriately.

4. As the major share of energy in this world depends upon the natural resources hence it is important that these resources must be preserved and used judiciously.

These are some of the reasons for which the goal 'Responsible Consumption and Production' has been created so that people can not only consume but also preserve all the essential resources that are needed for the development of the nation.

12.2 Targets of the goal of 'Responsible Consumption and Production':

Below mentioned are the targets of this goal which if achieved properly can result in its successful accomplishment:

1. **Reduction in the waste generation:** By the year 2030 there must be a reduction in the waste generation on the global level which can easily be done with the help of following processes, recycling, prevention, reusing etc.

2. **Encouraging companies to work towards sustainable development:** Various companies especially large and transitional ones must work towards the sustainable development and adopt congruent practices, not only this they must integrate the information of sustainability into their regular reporting cycles.

3. **Promoting Sustainable Lifestyles:** By 2030 people must be well aware of the practices which can help them live a

harmonious life and this cannot be done without working on the Global Goals.

4. **Looking after sustainable tourism:** Virtuous tools and processes must be developed in order to monitor sustainable tourism which is responsible for the creation of myriad jobs and promotion of the local culture of any city or country.

These are only a few of the targets, there are many other which can help in the achievement of goal ' Responsible Consumption and Production'.

12.3 Accomplishing the goal of ' Responsible Consumption and Production'

As mentioned above, we must be aware of different practices which can help us in preserving various resources while paying attention towards the production and consumption as well. Following are the solutions which can help us in accomplishing this goal:

1. Alternative sources of energy must be used because they don't generate harmful gases that are responsible for the damage caused to the ozone layer. Moreover, such resources aren't expensive and can be renewed easily.

2. More trees must be planted as trees and vegetation are responsible for the sustainability of ecosystem. They are also a great source of habitat for wildlife.

3. Judicious ways must be practiced in order to conserve water in homes.

4. Industrial waste must be treated in order to prevent thermal as well as chemical pollution of water.

5. Rainwater harvesting must be done in order to preserve water, this can also help in more water consumption during dry seasons.

6. Energy must be consumed as much as possible and for this some of easiest yet easily forgettable practices must be followed

without fail such as, switching off lights when not in use, unplugging various electrical appliances when they aren't being used etc.

7. Use of biogas instead of LPG must be encouraged in homes for the purpose of saving the depletion of oil reserves.

8. Wastes must be recycled and reused as this will enhance the remanufacturing of materials that have already been used.

9. Using electronic mails is another great way of saving paper and hence must be brought into practice.

10. Use of plastic bags must be stopped.

11. Old pieces of furniture must be either reused or donated to charity instead of being disposed of, this will reduce the wastage of wood.

12. Special attention must be paid to save and preserve our national heritage.

12.4 Student's involvement in the promotion of goal ' Responsible Consumption and Production'

Students with the help of their teachers or mentors must promote the significance of this goal by conducting and being a part of the following activities:

1. Create a campaign and run it in your school and surrounding areas asking people to abolish the use of plastic bags. Make it immensely informative so that best results can be achieved.

2. This is an interactive activity wherein students can spread awareness on saving the environment. Students can use their own creativity in order to make this activity informative and interesting.

3. Potluck sessions must be conducted in the classroom wherein students can learn the art of caring and sharing by having lunch

together instead of consuming it individually. At the same time, they must be encouraged to avoid the wastage of food.

4. An exhibition must be conducted in school in order to promote the cause of reusing and recycling of waste materials.

SUSTAINABLE DEVELOPMENT **GOALS**

17 GOALS TO TRANSFORM OUR WORLD

#SDGSketch

is a project by @Club17Africa http://club17africa.org in collaboration with @xlonirax and @DrMinaOgbanga

GOAL 13: Take urgent action to combat **climate change** and its impacts

Strengthen resilience and adaptive capacity to climate-related hazards and natural disasters in all countries

Improve education, awareness-raising and institutional capacity on climate change mitigation, adaptation, impact reduction and early warning

Integrate climate change measures into national policies, strategies and planning

Implement development countries commitment to United Nations Framework on Climate Change to mobilize jointly $100 billion/year by 2020 to fully operationalize the Green Climate Fund

Promote mechanisms for raising capacity for effective climate change-related planning and management in least developed countries

Developed Countries

Green Climate Fund $100 Bin
One hundred billions

Climate Change Planning & Management

Climate Change

GOAL 13: CLIMATE ACTION

The changes in climate these days is a threat to our entire civilisation which cannot be denied due to any reason. The outcome of these changes is very much visible and causing harm to this planet enormously. It is nothing else but statistical distribution of various weather patterns and is a global challenge these days, the most common way in which these changes are being experienced is the heat which is being generated in this planet. As the temperature is rising in different areas, it is getting difficult for certain animals and species to bear the heat and therefore they are not able to survive and are getting extinct. Not only animals, each year a lot of children and people are losing their life because they are not able to cope up with the climatic changes.

The main reason of earth being adversely affected and facing bad climatic condition is that since 150 years humans are getting themselves in activities which are releasing harmful gases into the atmosphere of earth and hence, in turn, are causing increase in the temperature. These changes in the climate are affecting wildlife on an enormous level, although there are many animals that are being affected due to these changes however mostly polar bears are being affected by them. The farming communities are also being adversely affected due to these changes as extreme heat is resulting in heavy rainfalls, floods etc which is causing harm to various crops and vegetation, especially in the developing countries. Due to this most of the farmers have started using cheap chemicals in order to harvest their crops and earn more money.

This goal aim towards encouraging people to get involved in activities that can augment the climatic conditions and ease out the pain of myriad people and beings across the globe.

13.1 Significance of the goal 'Climate Change'

Following are the points which reflect upon the significance of this goal:

1. Getting hold and rid of climate changes, in other words, global warming can bring in an amazing transformation on this planet.

2. Crops and vegetation can be saved which in turn can help us consume healthy and extremely fresh vegetables.

3. The life on earth can be saved once climatic conditions are improved. Not only this, it can improve the environment amazingly.

4. Hence, it is essential for us to work on this goal so that necessary changes can be made to all those things that are causes behind the climate changes. This is not a man show and therefore numerous people must be encouraged to work towards this goal, it is then we'll be able to attain sustainability of this planet.

13.2 Targets of the goal 'Climate Change'

Following are the targets which if worked upon persistently can bring an amazing transformation in climate and environment which will be good for all the beings on this planet:

1. Proper planning must be done in order to create national policies and strategies which can control the climatic changes.

2. Education can be used as a tool in order to create awareness about climatic changes and how they can be controlled. People must be encouraged to do justice to the environment so that it can be saved and stay protected, it's only then it will be able to do justice to all the beings, their life, and their existence.

13.3 Accomplishing the goal 'Climate Change'

Till the time we'll achieve this goal the world will not get relief from the harm caused by climate these days, hence following things can be done in order to accomplish it appropriately:

1. Talk to your friends, relatives, colleagues, neighbours etc and discuss how this planet is being adversely affected. Not only this together you can find out solutions which can help you to work towards this goal efficiently.

2. Invest money in energy saving appliances as this will reduce harmful gases being released into the air and keep the environment clean and fresh.

3. Water waste must be reduced and proper measures must be taken in order to keep the water bodies clean.

4. Use LED bulbs on a regular basis as they use up to 80 percent less energy than other conventional incandescents and can also be cheap in the long run.

5. Fuel-efficient vehicles must be used as they do not cause pollution in the air.

These are some of the common things which can be done in order to save the environment and improve climatic conditions however you can look for other solutions which can help you to work towards this goal.

13.4 Student's involvement in order to promote the goal 'Climate Change'

1. Students with the help of their teachers or mentors need to promote the significance of this goal by conducting and being a part of the following activities:

2. **Recycling Campaign:** Students must be encouraged to be a part of recycling activities wherein they'll be required to recycle

paper, plastic, metal etc. The articles recycled can be displayed in school in order to encourage novices to support this goal.

3. **Drive to stay healthy:** Choose a day wherein all the students can get involved in a cycling activity in order to promote the cause of using vehicles that don't cause air pollution.

4. **Be a veggie for a week:** Take a pledge with your teachers and fellow students that nobody will consume non-veg for a week, try and do this activity once in a month in order to see the best results.

SUSTAINABLE DEVELOPMENT **GOALS**

17 GOALS TO TRANSFORM OUR WORLD

#SDGSketch

is a project by @Club17Africa http://club17africa.org in collaboration with @xLentrex and @DrMinaOgbanga

GOAL 14: Conserve and sustainably use the oceans, seas and marine resources for sustainable development

By 2025 Prevent and significantly reduce marine pollution of all kinds

Provide access for small-scale artisanal fishers to marine resources and markets

By 2020 sustainably manage and protect marine and coastal ecosystems to avoid significant adverse impacts

By 2020 effectively regulate harvesting and end overfishing, illegal, unreported and unregulated fishing

By 2020 conserve at least 10% of coastal and marine areas

10%

By 2020 prohibit certain forms of fisheries subsidies which contribute to overcapacity and overfishing

Increase scientific knowledge, develop research capacity and transfer marine technology taking into account Intergovernmental Oceanographic Commission guidelines

Minimize and address the impact of ocean acidification, including through scientific cooperation at all levels

By 2030 increase economic benefits to Small Islands developing States and least developed countries from the sustainable use of marine resources

Enhance the conservation and sustainable use of oceans and their resources by implementing international law as reflected in UNCLOS

GOAL 14 : LIFE BELOW WATER

Healthy water bodies like oceans, rivers, and seas are essential for our existence, as you must be aware that around 70 percent of our planet is covered with water and everybody who's living on earth depends on the water bodies for food, energy and water. Despite of understanding its importance we have done all that is possible to damage the water bodies and other precious resources. It is high time that we now start working towards protecting them in an utmost manner if we really wish to enjoy living on a sustainable planet. We must stop polluting the water bodies by disposing off waste and congruent chemicals and materials in them, not only this we must also work towards eliminating pollution, overfishing and should manage the marine life around the world. If we look at the present condition we'll realise that 30 percent of the fish stocks have been overexploited and 40 percent of the oceans is affected by pollution which isn't good for the sustainable development of the environment.

14.1 Significance of the goal 'Life Below Water'

As mentioned above, we must work towards the development and improvement of our marine life so that the goal 'Life Below Water' can be achieved without any problem. Hence it is essential to understand the need and significance of this goal:

1. This goal encourages people to work towards the cleanliness of water which can help in preventing various diseases life infections, diarrhoea etc. which are caused due to impure water.

2. People will be motivated to do everything possible in order to keep the water bodies clean and pollution free.

3. Clean water is essential for our body as 55 to 70 percent of it is water, by working on his goal we'll be able to consume healthy water which can help us in keeping ourselves fit and healthy.

4. We need this goal in order to increase the quality of water so that healthy food can be cooked, if we wish to consume a healthy and nutritious diet then it is imperative that we use clean and fresh water while cooking food.

5. There are many people who are involved in water sports, impure water bodies will affect their health adversely hence it is essential to practice this goal so that these interesting activities can be enjoyed by enormous people.

6. Clean water is also responsible for the overall cleanliness of surroundings, hence it is a must to work towards keeping the water bodies clean and pure.

14.2 The targets of goal 'Life Below Water'

Following are the targets which must be attained in order to accomplish this goal:

1. **Reducing Marine Pollution:** By 2025 it is essential that marine pollution should be reduced if we wish to see a sustainable development on this planet.

2. **Reducing Ocean Acidification:** We need to minimise the acidification in the oceans with the help of various scientific innovations and cooperation at all levels.

3. **Sustainability in Fishing:** Unregulated and destructive fishing practices must be abolished and serious actions must be taken against those who involve themselves in such acts.

4. **Conserving Coastal and Marine Areas:** By the year 2020 at least 10 percent of the coastal and marine areas must be conserved with the help of stringent national and international laws based on appropriate and effective scientific research.

5. **Increasing Scientific Knowledge:** Awareness must be created among people so that they can understand their roles and responsibilities towards this goal and work accordingly. They must be familiarised with various methods which can help them in keeping the marine life safe and clean in their respective countries.

These are only a few of the targets, there are many more which students need to do some research upon and create effective solutions based on them to promote this goal appropriately.

14. 3   Accomplishing the goal 'Life Below Water'

Here are few of the steps which can be taken in order to accomplish this goal in an utmost manner:

1. Reducing the use of plastic can help in the elimination, most of the plastic that is thrown in the water isn't able to fish out and spread decay in water hence we need to be careful before throwing it in any of the water bodies.

2. It's better to get involved in activities like re-using or recycling as they prevent in things being disposed of unnecessarily.

3. Oil which is not good to use must not be thrown in the sinks and instead be disposed of in the garbage. You can also collect oil in a bottle and throw it in garbage or recycle it.

4. Cleaning chemicals are really dangerous and should not be thrown in the water bodies.

5. Throwing away medicines in water or flushing them down isn't a good practice and must be abolished.

6. Use environment-friendly detergents and soaps, though they are a little expensive but prevent water pollution.

These are a few of the tips, students are expected to do some research work and find out more which can help them to work towards this goal.

14.4 Student's involvement in promoting the goal 'Life Below Water'

Students with the help of their teachers or mentors need to promote the significance of this goal and encourage their peers to work towards it by conducting and being a part of the following activities:

1. **Say 'NO' to Wastage:** The waste on land is usually dumped into water, hence create an awareness campaign wherein you can encourage your fellow students and people living in the surrounding areas. A street show on this can also be a good idea to spread awareness about this topic.

2. **Clean Up Project:** With the help of your teachers and mentors create a cleaning project for local rivers or waterbodies.

Find out more activities on this and perform them involving as many students as possible for the purpose of promoting and supporting this goal.

SUSTAINABLE DEVELOPMENT GOALS #SDGSketch

17 GOALS TO TRANSFORM OUR WORLD

is a project by @Club17Africa http://club17africa.org in collaboration with @Lantrax and @DrMinaOgbanga

GOAL 15: Protect, restore and promote sustainable use of terrestrial ecosystems, sustainably manage forests, combat desertification and halt and reverse land degradation and halt biodiversy loss

By 2020 promote the implementation of sustainable management of all types of forests

By 2030 ensure the conservation of mountain ecosystems, including their biodiversity

By 2020 ensure the conservation, restoration and sustainable use of terrestrial and inland fresh-water ecosystems

Reduce the degradation of natural habitats

Take urgent action to end poaching and trafficking of protected species

Promote fair and equitable sharing of the benefits arising from the utilization of genetic resources

By 2020 introduce measures to prevent the introduction and reduce the impact of alien species

Integrate ecosystem and biodiversity value in national and local planning

By 2030 combat desertification and restore degraded land and soil

Financial Resources to:
• conserve and sustainably use ecosystems and biodiversity
• sustainable forest management
• combat poaching and traffic of protected species

GOAL 15 : LIFE ON LAND

This goal focusses on protecting, restoring and promoting the sustainable use of terrestrial ecosystems and managing forests. It also puts emphasis on taking care of various creatures and beings that are living on this planet, human life on earth is as important as the existence of oceans, rivers and other water bodies and is important for the economic development. 30 percent of earth's surface is covered with forests and provide habitat to myriad species, not only this, they are essential for clean air and water and are responsible for the changes that are taking place in the climate. However, it is very sad to know that at present out of the 8300 known breeds around 8 percent are extinct and 22 percent are at a risk of extinction.

The purpose of this goal is to restore and protect the forests, wetlands, drylands, wildlife, and mountains by 2030 which needs to be done in order to sustain the natural habit for different beings and species. Approximately 2.6 million people are depended directly on the agriculture in order to earn a living which needs to be sustained and not destroyed due to numerous hazardous factors.

15.1 Significance of the goal 'Life on Land'

If we wish to see a sustainable development on this planet then it is essential that we understand the significance of all the global goals, so let's look at the importance of goal 'Life on Land':

1. We need to take care of the forests so that various species do not have to lose their habitat.

2. The world is full of beautiful species which need to be protected in order to sustain its beauty hence working on this goal will enable us to prevent the extinction of various species and animals.

3. Various undesired climatic changes can be prevented if we will work upon this goal and save trees and forests.

15.2 Targets of the goal 'Life on Land'

Every individual needs to contribute to the achievement of the global goals it's only then they can be achieved. Following are the targets which need to be achieved for the purpose of successful completion of this goal:

1. **Protect Natural Habitats:** Significant actions must be taken in order to protect the habitats of various beings and species on earth and must put a halt on the loss of biodiversity and by 2030 the extinction of threatened species must be controlled.

2. **Forest Management:** Necessary steps must be taken in order to protect the forests and more focus must be put on conservation and reforestation so that they can be saved.

These are the most important targets which need to be worked upon however apart from these there are myriad other targets which must be considered and worked upon seriously to attain this goal successfully.

15.3 Accomplishment of the goal 'Life on Land'

Now that we have understood the need and importance of this goal, let's look at various measures which can help us in accomplishing this goal:

1. We must volunteer and support organisations that are working towards this goal and striving hard to protect forests and wildlife on a global level.

2. Conducting ecological surveys can help us in creating and establishing a congruent database.

3. Rainforests must be protected as they generate a good amount of oxygen.

4. The plants in rainforests cure different type of illnesses and also regulate our climate hence it is essential to save them. Billions of species will die if rainforests will be destroyed.

5. Different efficient policies and strategies must be developed in order to protect the flora and fauna on a global level.

6. Biodiversity and natural resources must be protected in order to achieve this goal.

15.4 Student's Involvement in promoting the goal 'Life on Land'

Students with the help of their teachers or mentors need to promote the significance of this goal and encourage their peers to work towards it by conducting and being a part of the following activities:

1. Students must be taken to Zoos, Aquarium, National Parks wherein they can see the condition of various species and animals and can prepare a report on the same. This report must be shared with various organisations that are working towards their welfare so that they can come up with realistic solutions for improvement.

2. Share your concern towards nature and wildlife with your peers and family and take a pledge to do everything possible in order to protect them.

3. Take a pledge in your school that nobody will buy anything that's created from the skin of endangered animals or species.

4. Conduct a 'Plant a Tree' drive with the help of your teachers and mentors and encourage people to take care of nature and environment, this will also help in the reduction of pollution.

SUSTAINABLE DEVELOPMENT GOALS

#SDGSketch

17 GOALS TO TRANSFORM OUR WORLD

is a project by @Club1fAfrica http://club1fAfrica.org in collaboration with @xlontrex and @DrTrinaOgbanga

GOAL 16: Promote peaceful and inclusive societies for sustainable development, provide access to justice for all and build effective, accountable and inclusive institutions at all levels

Reduce all forms of violence and related death rates everywhere

End abuse, exploitation, trafficking and all forms of violence against and torture of children

By 2030 reduce illicit financial and arms flows and combat all forms of organized crimes

Ensure equal access to justice for all

By 2030 provide legal identity for all including birth registration

Ensure responsive, inclusive, participatory and representative decision making at all levels

Broaden and strengthen the participation of developing countries in the institutions at global level

Strengthen relevant national institutions including through international cooperation for building capacity to prevent violence and combat terrorism and crime

Reduce corruption and bribery in all their forms

Develop effective, accountable and transparent institutions at all levels

Ensure public access to information and protect fundamental freedom

Promote and enforce non discriminatory laws and policies for sustainable development

Info: httns://sustainabledevelopment.un.org/sdg16

GOAL 16: PEACE, JUSTICE AND STRONG INSTITUTIONS

We need to live in a society wherein compassion, justice, humanity are the major attributes so that every person living there can feel safe and happy and that's what sustainable development goals aim at. With the help of these goals we can create virtuous institutions that can add on in the growth of the nation and prove themselves as great assets instead of burdening liabilities, and they should be strong enough so that they can be provided with an opportunity and responsibility of providing justice and maintaining peace all around on a global level.

Violence is perhaps the most destructive threat to the growth and development of any nation and various countries worldwide. There are different forms of violence out of which crime and sexual and gender-based violence have become extremely common these days. Hence, this goal aims at the promotion of peaceful and just societies and institutions for the purpose of sustainable development and supports the cause of providing justice for all with the help of governance and judicial systems which are responsible for the guarantee of human rights, security and law and order.

The initial step of creating such a society is by offering equal rights to all the individuals without any discrimination, and special attention must be paid to those who are living under any sort of physical, emotional or mental threat and are not able to enjoy their basic freedom.

There are approximately 10 million people worldwide who have been denied a nationality and rights related to the same. 603 million women live in those countries where domestic violence is not considered as a crime, this goal can help such people in getting their rights and justice against everything which is not letting them the life they deserve to live.

16.1   Significance of the goal ' Peace, Justice and Strong Institutions':

Following are the points which reflect upon the significance of this goal and encourage people to work on it for the purpose of creating a safe, compassionate and just society:

1. This goal promotes the cause of giving equal rights to all the individuals which will give them an opportunity to live freely in their country and enjoy their rights appropriately.

2. We need this goal so that any sort of crime can be eliminated from various countries on a global level and the world can become extremely peaceful and safe for all.

3. This goal holds the potential of building strong institutions which can offer justice to all those who need it the most.

16.2 Targets of the goal 'Peace, Justice and Strong Institutions'

Below given are the targets which if accomplished successfully can bring an amazing transformation in all the countries across the globe:

1. By 2030 strong policies and practices must be developed which can reduce or eliminate any sort of crime from cities and countries worldwide. This is essential for their growth as well as the safety and security of those living there. Not only this, all sorts of violence must be put to an end by the desired deadline.

2. Any sort of child exploitation or abuse must be put to an end, not only this trafficking and violence against children must be stopped.

3. Proper laws must be promoted on the national and international levels and equal justice for all must be ensured by all the respective institutional and government bodies.

4. Strong laws and policies must be created in order to stop such activities to take place in different countries and cities worldwide.

5. Relevant national institutions and international cooperations must be strengthened in order to build excellent capacity at all levels, especially in the developing countries in order to prevent crime and combat terrorism.

6. Such sort of laws and policies must be enforced so that the targets pertaining to sustainable development can be achieved successfully.

16.3 Accomplishing the goal 'Peace, Justice and Strong Institutions'

Now that we have understood various facts related to this goal along with the targets, it's time to look at different ways which can help us in achieving this goal efficiently:

1. Appropriate solutions and methods must be created in order to tackle the crime and congruent activities.

2. Virtuous neighbourhood activities must be conducted in order to bring people closer and together so that they can support each other and together can fight all that is not working out for their good.

3. Improving the local environment can also help in reducing the crime rate and increasing the chances of any country attaining peace easily.

4. Community walks is a great way of promoting equality and justice, hence these drives must be conducted on a regular basis in order to attain justice and equality for all.

5. All the countries and cities worldwide must create and follow a 'No Violence' policy in order to make themselves strong and safe.

16.4 Student's Role in promoting the goal 'Peace, Justice and Strong Institutions'

Students with the help of their teachers or mentors need to promote the significance of this goal and encourage their peers to work towards it by conducting and being a part of the following activities:

1. With the help of your teachers and mentors get in touch with your local and national authorities and ask them to help you conduct various initiatives which can work towards the welfare of society and planet.

2. Invite a speaker in your school or ask any of your teachers to take a session of all the students and explain them about their rights so that they can become well familiarised with the same and use them in an utmost manner.

3. Create weekly public posts on any burning issue related to sustainable development and circulate it with the help of social media or any other mean that can help you reach masses.

SUSTAINABLE DEVELOPMENT GOALS

#SDGSketch

17 GOALS TO TRANSFORM OUR WORLD

is a project by @Club17Africa http://club17africa.org in collaboration with @xlontrex and @DrMinaOgbanga

GOAL 17: Strengthen the means of implementation and revitalize the global partnership for sustainable development

FINANCE

- Mobilize additional financial resources for developing countries
- Domestic resource mobilization
- Domestic capacity for tax and other revenue collection
- Developed Countries to implement fully their official Development Assistance Commitments
- Adopt and implement investment promotion regimes for least developed countries
- Assist developing countries in attaining long-term debt sustainability

TRADE

- Increase the EXPORT of Developing Countries
  - UNIVERSAL
  - RULES-BASED
  - OPEN
  - NON DISCRIMINATORY
  - EQUITABLE MULTILATERAL
- Implement duty-free and quota-free market access on a lasting basis for all Least Developed Countries

TECHNOLOGY

- Environmentally sound Technologies
  - Transfer
  - Develop
  - Diffuse
  - Disseminate
- Access to:
  - Cooperation
    - International
    - Regional
  - Science
  - Technology
  - Innovation
- Operationalize
  - Enabling Tech
  - Science
  - Tech Bank

International Support

CAPACITY-BUILDING

Developing Countries

- Global partnership for Sustainable Development to achieve SDGs in all countries

SYSTEMIC ISSUES

- Respect country's policy space and leadership to establish and implement policies for poverty eradication & SD
- Enhance policy coherence
- Enhance global macroeconomic stability
- By 2020 enhance capacity-building support to Developing Countries
- Promote public, public-private and civil society partnership
- By 2030 build on existing initiatives to develop measurements of progress on Sustainable Development

Info @ http://illustratingsustainabledevelopment.org/6.17

GOAL 17: PARTNERSHIPS FOR THE GOALS

Sustainable Development Goals can be accomplished and realised with the help of virtuous global partnerships and can be met when we all work together. In order to achieve the innovative technological development the support of international investments is needed, not only for this, we need its involvement for the purpose of attaining the access of fair trade and market especially for those countries that are on developing stage. We all dream of a safe and peaceful world however need to understand that we all need to be equally supportive, compassionate, passionate and above all must be willing to cooperate with each other, it's only then we'll be able to build a stronger home for all.

Although there have been some positive developments recently, however, there still is a high need for partnership and cooperation in order to achieve the Sustainable Development Goals successfully. When we talk about partnerships and cooperation it means that all individuals must mobilise and share their knowledge and expertise with each other, instead of pulling each other down we need to work together and rise higher if wish to see sustainable development on a global level. Also, it is imperative to collectively work upon and come up with some of the most effective solutions for technological issues along with the enhancement of financial resources, especially in developing countries.

17.1 Significance of 'Partnerships for the goals'

This goal is important because without forming effective partnerships and collaborations we will not able to achieve the Sustainable Goals easily. All the 17 goals are interconnected however if we really wish to attain them then we would need contribution and participation of every individual and at each level. Hence, this particular goal works upon creating proficient partnerships that can help in the growth of the nation as well as make all the countries well equipped with all that is necessary for a healthy and prosperous living.

17.2 Targets of 'Partnerships for the goals'

Following targets must be attained in order to form appropriate partnerships for the goals:

1. **Mobilising the resources to augment the revenue collection:** Effective international support must be given to countries that are on developing stage so that they can improve their domestic capacity.

2. **Arranging financial resources for developing countries:** We need to arrange and organise additional funds and financial resources with the help of various means and multiple sources for all the developing countries.

3. **Sustainability of Debt:** Help must be provided to the developing countries so that they can attain long-term debts with the help of coordinated policies, not only this there must be certain debt relief measures created for the poor countries so that they can reduce their debt distress.

4. **Investing in the least developed countries:** Undeveloped countries need more attention and assistance so that it can match up with the pace of developed ones. Hence, it is imperative that more investment must be put into the development of these countries in order to enhance their condition.

5. **Knowledge Sharing:** All the individuals from various fields must come together and share their knowledge and expertise with each other so that we can build a strong and prosperous nation.

6. **Innovation must be strengthened in the least developed countries:** Myriad innovative measures and methods must be created in order to improve the condition of countries that are on developing stage.

These are some of the targets, there are many other which need to be worked upon if we wish to see a proper Sustainable Development in the world.

17.3 Accomplishment of 'Partnerships of Goals'

Like stated above, this goal can be attained with proper collaboration and forming good partnerships. In short, the achievement of this goal depends upon how well every person contributes towards the development of undeveloped countries and enhance the existence of developed ones. This goal strongly believes that Sustainable Development can never be attained alone and we all need to come forward and support each other for attaining it successfully.

17.4 Student's involvement in promoting 'Partnerships of Goals'

Students with the help of their teachers or mentors need to promote the significance of this goal and encourage their peers to work towards it by conducting and being a part of the following activities:

1. **Volunteering for Global Goals:** The students must get in touch with organisations and NGO's that are working towards the Global Goals and offer a helping hand to them in promoting and supporting their cause.

2. **Donation Box:** A Donation Box must be created in your school premises and students must be encouraged to donate any amount as per their wish which would go to various organisations that are working towards the well being of the country and it's beings & residents. This amount must be donated for a good cause.

3. **Brain Storming Activities:** Brain storming sessions must be conducted on various global issues and students must plan activities pertaining to them so that the problems around these topics can be eliminated and awareness about the same must be created in end number of people.

Useful Resources

We have listed few useful resources that will help you garner the Education for sustainable development in our future generations and will also help you in equipping yourselves and your colleagues with upto date knowledge and skills required

- 17 Goals to Transform our World https://www.un.org/sustainabledevelopment/

- Exemplary Classroom Resources by teachers for teachers http://resources4rethinking.ca/en/what-is-esd

- Education for Sustainable Development by UNESCO https://en.unesco.org/themes/education-sustainable-development

- Teach for SDGs http://www.teachsdgs.org/

- Partnership for 21st Century Learning http://www.p21.org/news-events/p21blog/2282-building-a-better-world-six-strategies-for-engaging-the-sustainable-development-goals-in-the-classroom

- Global Schools Program https://www.globalschoolsprogram.org/

- World's Largest Lesson http://worldslargestlesson.globalgoals.org/

- SDG Teaching Tools & Child friendly material https://www.unicef.org/agenda2030/69525_82235.html

- Practical Actions https://practicalaction.org/global-goals

- Resources for teaching the Sustainable Development Goals https://filmsfortheplanet.com/project/resources-for-teaching-the-sustainable-development-goals/

- Free online courses from the worlds leading experts on SDGs https://sdgacademy.org/

- UNICEF Kid Power https://schools.unicefkidpower.org/kid-power-ups#.W6HpPBNLiL8

- Curriculum framework: Education for Sustainable Development https://www.globaleslernen.de/sites/default/files/files/link-elements/

curriculum_framework_education_for_sustainable_development_ba
rrierefrei.pdf

- Sustainable Development Goals Reports & Resources http://
www.unfoundation.org/features/globalgoals/the-global-goals-
reports-and-resources.html

- Online courses on Sustainable Development Goals https://
www.class-central.com/report/united-nations-sdg-courses/

- Achieving Sustainable Development an online course https://
www.futurelearn.com/courses/achieving-sustainable-development

- eCourses by UNITAR http://www.unitar.org/pillars/cross-fertilizing-
knowledge/2030-agenda-online-training-programmes

About Authors

HIMANNSHU SHARMA

Himannshu Sharma is a social educational entrepreneur who is mentoring various educational institutions around the world and helping them grow globally. He is the founder of various social initiatives including Project Education, GEAERD and is leading various global social organisations by being in their board of directors. He is an expert & mentor to educational institutions in UN relations, Educational Grants, SDGs, Leadership and Green Infrastructure. To know more about him visit https://about.me/hsharmaofficial

You may also connect with him on LinkedIn: https://www.linkedin.com/in/hsharma23/

TINA SOBTI

Tina Sobti is a visionary educator who started her journey to be the catalyst of change for masses.

She is an avid reader, learner and explorer who believes in experiencing new learnings, courses, places and her attitude has made her do Clinical Hypnotherapy, a metaphysical science and she regularly applies her knowledge in making teaching learning mechanism more interesting and innovating for her students.

To know more about her visit https://about.me/tinasobti

You may also connect with her on LinkedIn: https://www.linkedin.com/in/tina-sobti/

Feel free to write to our editorial team for any feedback

editor@projecteducation.co

https://projecteducation.co

Made in United States
North Haven, CT
09 September 2023

41344630R00075